SEE AND FEEL

THE
INSIDE MOVE THE OUTSIDE

D1567673

"Golf while not an easy game, above all is a game of ease. You are probably saying, golf may be easy for some people, but it is hard for me. I have no concentration, or I miss that ball, and I have to give it all I got or it won't ride. If there is such a thing as easy golf, there must be some formula for acquiring it. There has to be a positive method of overcoming my faults . . ."

— Alex Morrison

YES, THERE IS A FORMULA —

"THE INSIDE MOVES THE OUTSIDE"

Michael Hebron

AUTHOR'S BIOGRAPHY

Attained Master Professional Status	1985
Golf Professional of the Year (Metropolitan PGA)	1982
Horton Smith Award (Metropolitan PGA)	1981
PGA National Academy of Golf, Instructor	
Appointed to the National Golf Foundation Staff	1980
Appointed to the National PGA Education Staff	1976
PGA National Teaching Workshop, Instructor	
Elected to the Metropolitan PGA Honor Roll	1975
Writes Golf Instructions for National Publications	
Writes Golf Tips for Newspapers	
Holds Course Record (64) at Smithtown Landing	
Director of Golf at Smithtown Landing Country Club	
Vice-President of Metropolitan PGA	1980-1985

Has directed Adult Golf Schools, Workshops, Seminars, and Junior Golf Camps.

Clinics given throughout the country at Clubs, Colleges, High Schools, Elementary Schools, Adult Education Classes, Civic Groups, 1986 U.S. Open, and many other Tournaments.

"Congratulations! 'See and Feel the Inside Move the Outside' . . . It is certainly equal to or better than any thesis on the subject of teaching I've ever seen turned into the PGA . . ."

Joseph A. O'Brien
Director of PGA Education

"Obviously, Mike has studied and worked hard to acquire the knowledge and research to write this book, and deserves a lot of credit. In my opinion, it's very good. Any golfer could get some good thoughts from it. It was a pleasure to read."

Hank Haney
Renowned Golf Coach

"Mike Hebron rates at the top of the field as a student of the game, teacher, player, and perhaps most important for all of us a COMMUNICATOR!"

"As one of the best minds in golf, his results on the teaching tee are remarkable and permanent."

"His ideas, concepts and insights into the swing herein 'The Inside Moves the Outside,' are uniquely presented, are not only valid, but are important and helpful for golfers at all skill levels of the game."

Dave Pelz
Renowned in Golf Research and Shot Game Coaching

Dear Mike,

I want you to know our discussion about the golf swing has helped me a lot. I hope that I see you again soon, you are very knowledgeable about the swing, but not only that, you are good at presenting your ideas in a way that makes it easy for the mind of the student to understand. I made my first check on the LPGA tour the next week.

Charlotte Montgomery
(an LPGA tour professional, and winner of top amateur tournaments)

Dear Mike,

You're a real class act! The Clinic on Sunday was one of the highlights of the day.

Everyone was impressed with, not only your knowledge of the game, but your ability to present this knowledge in a way that makes sense to the rankest beginner.

These qualities alone are the mark of a fine teacher, but you add to them a sense of a dedication that is outstanding.

Don Hicks

Mike,

I can't tell you how much your ideas and concepts of the swing are helping me. Your insights will improve not only my game, but the games of those who come to me for help. You gave me the answers. Now I can use them and be successful.

Jerry Scott
Golf Professional

Mike Hebron's "The Inside Moves The Outside" presents to its readers such a concise conception and understanding of the golf swing, that any mystique about the swing is forever and immediately swept away.

One of the chapters "See it in other sports," is a book in itself.

Bill Strausbaugh
National PGA of America Professional of the Year

Observations By Professionals After
Mike Hebron's Presentation At Some PGA Schools

- "Keeps lessons from being boring!"

- "Great Communicator!"

- "Ability to communicate is excellent!"

- "My overall reaction to his presentation, it cannot improve!"

- "Effective communicator, excellent!"

- "Gave a lot of helpful information about teaching golf!"

- "His visual aids were excellent!"

- "Super job!"

ACKNOWLEDGMENTS

I want to express my gratitude to several people who have helped make this book possible.

First, my thanks to all the golfers I have worked with over the years. I learned from all of them. When they were pleased with their progress, it gave me the encouragement to put my approach to paper.

I am most appreciative of the PGA of America Education Department, and the National Golf Foundation for the opportunity to give clinics and teach all over the country. Those assignments helped develop and test my ideas.

My thanks to my fellow PGA golf professionals, who took an interest and helped me grow as a person and a professional.

The membership at my club, Smithtown Landing Country Club on Long Island, has always played a part in any progress I have made in golf, and this book must be included.

I want to thank my friends and family. A special thanks to both for their support over the years.

Michael Hebron

FOREWORD

BELIEVE IT OR NOT

    A.   The backswing is only a few inches long as is the front swing.

    B.   Bad shots or swings happen ONLY when centrifugal force stops or is interrupted.

    C.   You should not try to finish your swing facing the target

    D.   To have a late release, to retain the angle or to hit late, golfers with sound swings do nothing with their hands and arms.

    E.   The 'how to' in golf is important but the FEEL of how to is more important.

    F.   Our nervous system is more important than the muscle system.

    G.   Balance is a result of a low center of gravity and counter balance.

WE ARE OFTEN MISLED BY THE TYPE OF INFORMATION STORED IN THE PERSONAL COMPUTER OF THE MIND'S EYE

    A.   Without question, the most important keys in golf are the *Concepts* and *Visualizations* of the swing that are stored in your mind's eye.

    B.   We can be misled in golf by what we feel and think we see.

    C.   We must learn to recognize the difference between a golfer's personal mannerisms and the actions and movements of a sound swing.

    D.   The golf swing that your body will try to make is based on what *Concepts* and *Visualizations* you have in your mind's eye.

    E.   Understanding leads to a sound swing. The proper swing does not lead to understanding.

PHYSICAL TALENT IS IMPORTANT IN ANY SPORT, BUT IT IS TRULY INSIGNIFICANT IN COMPARISON TO THE MENTAL ASPECT OF LEARNING

    A.   The physical body cannot teach.

    B.   The body does not move on its own; movement happens for one of three reasons: reflexes, anticipation, or when the body receives a command message from the mind.

    C.   Your mind does not hit the ball, but it can stop the swing.

    D.   We must change on the inside first, then work on the outside.

    E.   We must learn how to train the mind.

    F.   We must learn that the right side of the brain is more important then the left (for golf).

SUCCESS AND PROGRESS WILL COME IN GOLF ONLY AFTER YOU WORK

"As I look back on those early days, I suppose that in my youthful mind, I was dimly aware that the quality of my game was going to be forever tied to the elements of sacrifice and personal discipline. Success is closely tied to determination, and that quality is not precisely related to native talent. I was a poor player and slow in attaining my goals, a late maturer they call it."

Ben Hogan

Table Of Contents

INTRODUCTION

We have enjoyed putting the information you are about to read together for you. It has taken several years, and I hope you enjoy it and find our suggestions and point of view helpful.

Golfers come in all sizes, from different backgrounds, all with athletic abilities found to be on levels from poor to excellent.

A goal of educators in any and all fields of instruction is to find different methods to help their students learn. Suggestions that help one student may not be of value to the next. This universal challenge to the teaching community does not by-pass golf instruction.

"Above all, we must recognize that the golf swing may be simple in theory, but the machine that performs it is very complicated: The great challenge to the teacher becomes the recognition and treatment of the individual differences in the MACHINE."
(Dr. Gary Wiren)

Over the years, a number of fine golf instruction books have been written. Some have come from well-known instructors, others from successful players. Our thoughts on golf are given here with encouragement that comes from several directions.

Encouragment came from Ben Hogan in the early 1950's when he said, "I hope my book will lead to future advances in our understanding of the game and in another 15 years, we will refine and extend our present knowledge of golf. In the future other men will have that pleasure." Another well-known leader in the world of golf instruction, Dr. Gary Wiren, said, "We must keep searching for new and better ways."

When looking at the sound swings of the last 50 years, you are going to find they are all very much alike. So when Ben Hogan and Dr. Wiren speak of "searching for new and better ways," and "refining or extending knowledge," it is not unreasonable to feel what they were hoping for was not NEW LAWS or PRINCIPLES of the golf swing, but new and different ways of communicating the laws and principles of the swing.

Encouragement has also come from my students and seeing the progress they have made. The Ladies' U.S. Open, the Men's U.S. Amateur, the U.S.G.A. Junior Boys, the U.S.G.A. Junior Girls, are tournaments that teenage golfers (who have played for only a few years) have played in over the last three years. High and low handicappers and professionals have also been golfers I have had the privilege of working with over the last 18 years.

Be aware that any progress a student makes is because of work. It is team work between you and your coach that produces the results that both are looking for. Students must also work on their own. Self-discovery is a big part of learning. A teacher or coach can impart knowledge, but skill must come from the student.

Successful teachers and coaches have been blessed with students who are willing to work. The famous Tommy Armour, when asked who was golf's greatest teacher answered, "It takes great learners to make great reputations for teachers, pupils who really want to learn, even if it means a slight mental effort and physical inconvenience." Any recognition that I have received is due largely to the work and effort my students have put into their games.

After work, the next step is for a student to have trust in his or her coach.

The final step in any successful learning environment may be the most obvious: the information a student receives must be worthwhile.

Learning to personally define and remember what you are feeling when you swing is an important step too. Indeed, a good coach and worthwhile information are necessary, but more importantly, coaches become very good when students apply themselves.

Suggestions that are made here are sound, but I don't have a government patent on their origin. No golf secrets here. What you may find, for better or worse, is some originality in the way information is shared with you. Our suggestions are based on the laws and principles of physics, math, and the structure of our bodies. The motions and actions you will be made aware of exist in all sound golf swings, and if I may say, "without exception."

We recognize that no two players swing the club in exactly the same manner. But a trained observer has learned to separate the personal mannerisms of a golfer from the set motions which are regarded as essential to playing the game. The actions and motions of a swing that are not personal mannerisms are found to be common in all sound swings. It is these actions and motions that we hope to give understanding and insight to.

Suggestions will be given as accurately as possible. Not with the hope that you can immediately perform them, but that you will have worthwhile concepts and visualizations that will give you a better understanding of a sound swing. Your body will start to learn and acquire the feel of sound movements only after you start to practice and work. You will not see progress until you work.

In addition to being asked to work, I am asking for your trust, in both me and the information to be shared. At this point you may want to, or find it helpful, to know more about me.

For many reasons it is a pleasure to be a golf professional, and I am sure you could list most of them. It is a broad based profession, and the rewards come from several directions. But it is the teaching and coaching segment that holds a special joy for me. If asked why, I am not sure I could be specific. I can tell you this — the responsibility of being asked to help someone try to make progress with their game is very serious to me. During some lessons it takes just a few minutes to tell what information can be helpful. On the other hand, there are lessons where you must take a much longer look.

The information and suggestions that you will receive here are given with the same responsibility I bring to any lesson tee. Again, there are no new golf swing secrets here; that would be misleading. What you will read are tips and suggestions that you can bring to your own PERSONAL STYLE. They may be given in a way that is new for you, but keep in mind, golfers with sound swings do not have secrets that they keep all to themselves.

For your convenience we have left a space for footnotes on each page of the book. At times you will find footnotes by me but it is my feeling you will enhance the value of the book by adding some of your own.

Information will not only come from my own point of view, but from discoveries and beliefs of other professionals and scientists. From time to time, quotes from other books and professionals will be used. This, we feel, is the best way to present suggestions that can make a difference in your game. The thoughts and ideas of today are based on and are expansions of information from past years. Ben Hogan and Bobby Jones' thoughts will be used more than some others. This happens for the best of reasons. Hogan and Jones were not only outstanding players, maybe the finest, but also outstanding students of the game. We know of no others who meet this very rare combination of talents.

Many books have presented instructional information in a way that tends to be "How to" or "This is how I do it," which is fine. Golf can and will vary a bit, even for champions, especially in the way the swing feels when it is in motion.

But it has not been uncommon for golfers, after reading one of these well-written books, for their progress to be short-lived or not what they expected. A book can be good at showing you "How I do it," but may not have communicated points I feel are the keys that can make a difference in the progress "YOUR" game is capable of.

Jack Nicklaus and Tom Watson have made some swing changes over the last few years. Some of the changes will be used as examples to help with your progress.

Learning is natural; it can be and should be fun. You learn and make progress if you think you can. You do have the natural resources and potential. If you think you can, there is a good chance you will. So together, let's make the effort.

Making suggestions through the written word is not an easy task for a teacher or student. It sure would help if we had a lesson tee available. But I am going to be very careful with what is written and how it is expressed, and I am confident you will gain worthwhile information that can help in the progress of your game.

It has been our experience that the approach to learning golf in this book has helped golfers at every level. I do not feel it is the only way. But we do feel, it may be the most uncomplicated approach that you could use for understanding and improving your game.

Part I

YOUR MIND'S EYE

I have long believed that if golfers could see a sound golf swing clearly in their "mind's eye" before they tried to make it, this would be the guarantee or key that was going to make the difference in the progress of their game.

Please believe that when you can mentally picture what you are trying to do, or are being asked to do, the task is more than half done. This is true not only in golf, but in any endeavor. We hope to provide information that can give you a clear understanding of what you would like to do with your body when making your swing. With an understanding of the swing in your "mind's eye," lessons taken in the future will be more helpful and the progress that is possible will come. In fact, the improvement will be dramatic.

Ben Hogan told us, "The average golfer's problem is not so much the lack of ability as it is a lack of knowledge about what he should be doing."

Bobby Jones talked in depth about the mind. "The one influence most likely to assure the satisfactory progression of the swing is clear visualization in the player's mind of movements. This can do more for a player than anything else he can possibly do, and I stress this point."

Jack Nicklaus felt that, "Many golfers probably do not understand cause and effect factors."

Alex Morrison, the most respected teacher of his time felt, "The excellence of your game will depend upon the extent to which your mind takes charge, and the way your body responds to its commands.

Alex wrote a book that was totally devoted to the use of the "mind's eye" and it was a topseller and considered a masterpiece.

The main tools of the mind's eye are Visualization and Conception. They are the two most important aids in playing successful golf. In other sports we may play or watch, reflexes and anticipation are the tools needed.

To anticipate correctly where an opponent will hit the tennis ball, to anticipate where the ball is about to be passed in basketball, to anticipate the kind of pitch about to be delivered, to anticipate the next play the quarterback will call . . . I could go on . . . but it is our ability to use our reflexes and anticipation skills that makes better performances in most sports. But this does not hold true for golf.

In golf our ability to make a sound swing is based on visualization and conceptions. It is how you see (before hand) the MOVEMENTS you would like to make with your body that can make the difference in your swing.

It can be a putt, a greenside chip, a tee shot. Better players have a better visualization of what they want to do with their bodies before they swing. Better players also remember the feel of the swing, good or bad.

Our bodies will not move on their own. You must BELIEVE this! Movement comes from one of three reasons: REFLEXES, ANTICIPATION, or when the body receives a MENTAL COMMAND MESSAGE. In golf, it is a mental message sent to the body through our nervous system that is responsible for the actions and movements that make up the swing.

A basketball foul shot and the bowling motion are the same. As you are about to start these two athletic movements, your mind will be telling your body what to do. There is no opponent causing movement.

We do not react in golf. You create the swing. The movements are not caused by a ball or the opponent's actions. They are a self-imposed creation, not a reaction or movement of anticipation. Keep in mind, the message sent can only be based on what information is stored in the personal computer of your mind. If you have poor concepts and visualizations, your swing is performing under the influence of a handicap.

We do not feel it is unfair to point out, when looking at the swing most golfers make, to assume they do not have the kind of worthwhile concepts and visualizations they should have.

I made some notes while having breakfast with the well known golf coach Chuck Hogan, the author of *Five Days to Golfing Excellence* (a book every serious golfer should own). Chuck was familiar with my work and I knew of his success in working with tour players Peter Jacobsen, Johnny Miller, Mary Beth Zimmerman, Barbara Mizrahie (to name a few) on the mental side of the game. Our breakfast turned into a wonderful three hour exchange of ideas. The following is from my notes:

GOLF IS A CREATIVE PROCESS

Your understanding makes the proper swing. The proper swing does not create understanding.

You can create when you gather information about a situation, reflect on it, and then react to it.

You respond efficiently *only* when you remain receptive to information being provided by the *target*. If you shift your attention to yourself, you take attention off the target.

EXAMPLE: Telling yourself you have not made a putt all day as you stand over your next putt is not the correct approach. You should address the putt, look at the target, and then make your swing.

Golf is both mental and physical. Your body *only* does what your brain commands. Your eyes do not see; your ears do not hear; your mouth does not taste; your fingers do not feel; your nose does not smell. It's your brain that deciphers all the information provided by your sensory organs. These body parts are merely receptors for brain information.

You are a Biocomputer - your brain is the computer hardware, your body is the print-out, and your images are the software. Your body will do what the software programs it to do.

Your body movements are always "efficient." Your body will only do what it has been told to do by your brain. When your swing produces a shot you are not happy with, please realize your brain produced that swing. The swing did not just happen, your body responded to the message your brain sent out, *"efficiently."*

Before going on, I have just stated in my view, that the most important keys in golf are the concepts and visualizations of the swing that are stored in your minds eye. After you have useful concepts and visualizations they must be put to use from a stance or posture that is correct and *does not* change during the swing.

When a sound swing is being influenced by the laws of motion, one reason their input would stop is a change in posture during the swing.

A change in posture during the swing may cause the angle of the spine to move, the center of gravity to change or your base of support to be altered (to mention only a few).

Any of these changes will destroy an otherwise sound swing by altering the plane or path of the clubhead.

A correct set-up that is not altered during the swing should be the goal of every golfer. (The spine is tilted, head or chin is up off the chest, the knees are flexed and buttocks out.)

HOW THE MIND'S EYE WORKS

Your brain should be thought of as a "split brain." It is made up of a left and right hemisphere, both with separate responsibilities when the brain is working. The California Institute of Techology has been one of the leaders in providing facts and information on the endless workings of the brain. Some of what will be shared with you here comes from their research.

The Left hemisphere works with VERBAL information, while the Right hemisphere works with VISUAL information. They are two different forms of information — they are not alike. It is my suggestion that we must learn to see the sound golf swing without being misled by what we are looking at. This can be accomplished by using the Right hemisphere more than the Left.

You have heard some good players say that they do not think (Left side verbal) about their swing when playing. Also, some fine instructors will state that it is possible to think (Left side verbal) too much when playing. I would strongly agree with both.

But, no one has ever suggested not to (Right side visual) picture, feel, or visualize what you would like to do beforehand in golf.

What we suggest to our students is to "stop" playing with words (Left side verbal) up-down-fast-in-out etc., and start to rely on (Right side visual) concepts, pictures, feels, and visualizations. This approach has been very successful with students at all levels.

It is much easier for most of us to follow a "Visual Suggestion," (show me how, and I will copy) then to try and follow written directions (first do this, then do that, then do this).

Learning to improve your golf game is going to be more than learning the physical skill. It is learning to use the right hemisphere to see and feel the golf swing that will lead to lasting improvements.

In the world of artists and painters, it is said the great ones can see better than average artists. They learn how to really see.

"The painter draws with his eyes, not with his hands. Whatever he sees, if he sees it clear, he can put down."

(Maurice Grosser)

"Learning to draw is really a matter of learning to see, to see correctly — and that means a good deal more than merely looking with the eyes." *(Kimon Nicolaides)*

Betty Edwards tells us, "Artists say that they feel alert and aware yet are relaxed and free of anxiety, experiencing a pleasurable, almost mystical activation of the mind." I think most golfers would like to be in this state of mind when playing.

In our approach to golf instruction, we tell our students that a round of golf is not one game, but 70, 80, or 90 separate times the mind must tell the body what to do, 70, 80, or 90 separate performances, 70, 80, or 90 separate pictures to be drawn. The game of golf is played by creating golf swings, and the better or clearer you can see that swing before you try to perform it, the better your chances are for success.

Most of the education you have been exposed to over the years has been geared to the Left hemisphere. In fact, it has been discovered that the Left hemisphere will take over the thinking process in most circumstances. Our approach in this book is different from other instruction books or school books you have used in the past. We are going to help you use and learn to trust the Right hemisphere, to make it stronger than the naturally dominant Left hemisphere.

Keep in mind that the thinking process happens in two modes, WORDS and PICTURES. It is our suggestion that you learn to play by mental pictures, not verbal suggestions that cannot be turned into a visualization.

"You should not concentrate, if it is taken to mean such a pulling of oneself together, such a fixing of the mind on the task at hand, such a tight-lipped determination to do one's best, that golf becomes a trial of nervous strength rather than a game."[1]

"I say that a golfer can only produce his true quality when he can play without concentrating (in a sense), when he can make his shots without clenching his teeth."[2]

"The good golfer feels his swing as all one piece. It is produced by a psycho-physical unison and its control is outside the mind of the player. Any control that is within the mind is subject to the state of the mind and is therefore unreliable."[3]

"Good golf, consistent golf, depends upon being able to shut out our mental machinery (with its knowledge of the difficulties of the shot, the state of the game, etc.) from those parts of us which play golf shots."[4]

1, 2, 3, 4 - Quotes by Percy Boomer

"Body muscles receive their instruction and initiative from the mind. The mind gets its information from the eyes. The eyes will register clearly in the mind the things to be accomplished. Thus, the mind may properly instruct the muscles on the things to be done if they are not misled.

— Seymor Dunn

Before going on with this book, write down how you swing, what you think about before you start, what you think about during the swing. Take the approach that you are giving someone instructions on "how to make a golf swing." Try to keep it short.

When I meet with someone for the first time, for me to be of any help, I must know what a student thinks about when making his/her swing. It's *The Starting Point* for a coach and student. This is a must.

What the student describes may be a very acceptable approach to the swing by any standards. But this golfer may be describing a swing that is very different from the way he/she actually swings (say one thing and do something else). Then too, after hearing students tell me what they think the swing should be or what they are trying to do, I may feel they do not have a worthwhile approach.

If you were to write about your swing *NOW*, I believe it could help you more than you may think. You will be able to refer back to your description as you read this book. Someone suggested that I write about my own swing very early in my professional career and it proved to be most helpful.

THE TWO MODES OF INFORMATION PROCESSING

Inside each of our skulls we have a double brain with two ways of knowing. The dualities and differing characteristics of the two halves of the brain and body, intuitively expressed in our language, have a real basis in the physiology of the human brain. Because the connecting fibers are intact in normal brains, we rarely experience at a conscious level conflicts revealed by the tests on split-brain patients.

Nevertheless, as each of our hemispheres gathers the same sensory information, each half of our brains may handle the information in different ways: the task may be divided between the hemispheres, each handling the part suited to its style. Or one hemisphere, often the dominant left, will "take over" and inhibit the other half. The left hemisphere alalyzes, abstracts, counts, marks time, plans step-by-step procedures, verbalizes, and makes rational statements based on logic. For example, "Given numbers a, b, and c — we can say that if a is greater than b, and b is greater than c, then a is necessarily greater than c." This statement illustrates the left-hemisphere mode: the analytic, verbal, figuring-out, sequential, symbolic, linear, objective mode.

On the other hand, we have a second way of knowing: the right hemisphere mode. We "see" things in this mode that may be imaginary — existing only in the mind's eye — or recall things that may be real (can you imagine your front door, for example?). We see how things exist in space and how the parts go together to make up the whole. Using the right hemisphere, we understand metaphors, we dream, we create new combinations of ideas. When something is too complex to describe, we can make gestures that communicate. Psychologist David Galin has a favorite example: try to describe a spiral staircase *without* making a spiral gesture. And using the right hemisphere we are able to draw pictures of our perceptions.

Dr. J. William Bergquist, a mathematician and specialist in the computer language known as APL, proposed in a paper given at Snowmass, Colorado, in 1977 that we can look forward to computers which combine digital and analog functions in one machine. Dr. Bergquist dubbed his machine "The Bifurcated Computer." He stated that such a computer would function similarly to the two halves of the human brain.

"The left hemisphere analyzes over time, whereas the right hemisphere synthesizes over space."
— Jerry Levy
"Psychobiological Implications of Bilateral Asymmetry"

WE ARE MISLED BY WHAT
WE THINK WE SEE AND FEEL

When video replay became available several years ago, all in professional golf were looking forward to the very real prospect of how we could help golfers get more out of their game by reshowing a swing only seconds after it was made. How wonderful. Surely this new tool would be a breakthrough for both the student and the teacher. But this was not to be.

It was not only my experience, (but that of other professionals) that golfers who could have been helped the most, did not take advantage of this new teaching aid. It was my impression that most golfers did not want to see a swing that was hitting shots they had been trying to improve for years. Most, I am sure, felt their swing had to be improved, but they failed to recognize how television replay could improve their visualization tenfold. There was a lack of understanding on how helpful concepts and visualizations are to the progress that golfers look for.

Repeating: *"Good players have a clear concept of what they want to do with their body in the mind's eye before they swing."*

Pictures do not lie. I do not know of one good golfer with a sound swing, who has not used pictures of themselves or of other top players to improve their own concepts and visualizations of the swing.

Alex Morrison told this story about Bobby Jones. "When Jones first saw slow motion pictures of his swing, he was astounded to note that the details of his swing when performed differed markedly from the swing he believed he was making. Bob would occasionally make statements regarding the execution of shots that were not consistent with what was actually taking place." Morrison went on, "I have motion pictures of Jones and other great players which shows conclusively that their own ideas of the swing and the actual swing they make are at wide variance."

Remember what you have just read. It may be one of the most important pieces of information a golfer could be made aware of. You cannot see your swing. For everyone, the swing will be different in feel than the way it actually looks. Until a golfer learns this, there will be a roadblock in making progress. Your feel can mislead and slow your progress. We are going to talk more about feel later, but an example of being misled is the length of the backswing.

I have asked students (at any level of ability) to put the club at the spot they feel or think it goes to at the top or end of their backswing. No one has ever put the club at their spot, no one, in all the years I have been teaching. After they are shown where their club actually travels to, it is met with disbelief. "I do not believe it," or "You have to be kidding!"

They have been misled by their feel. Most take the club back longer than they think. (Learn from this how easy it is to be fooled by what you think you are doing). To be misled by what you think you are seeing is also very common. Most golfers are not pointed where they think they are. Also, when looking at a fine player swing, you can be tricked. Seeing the club head move at 100 mph, creating lots of power, with the ball going considerable distance, the onlooker may think they are seeing a lot of athletic strength at work. This is not true, and they have been misled.

Listed are only a few examples of misconceptions, and if your mind's eye uses them as concepts or visualizations to base your swing and game on, golf will be much harder than it should be.

We are going to give you a new or different way of looking at the golf swing. These concepts and visualizations will be the foundation for progress you are capable of and have been looking for.

We feel there will be an understanding of the swing that you have not had before. It will NOW be easier for you to have a picture in your mind's eye of what you would like to do with your body before making the swing.

Learning about feel can also help with your visualization and concepts. In 1980, I sent a questionnaire to the men and women who play their respective tours, outstanding amateurs, and several club professionals who play tournament golf. Having friends in all those areas, I expected a good response and I was not disappointed. What I wanted to gather was information on what good players are feeling when they play, not how they play. What did they feel when they held the club? What did they feel at address? What did the backswing and the front swing feel like? At the end of the swing was there any special feel? What about the head? I also asked if they had any personal thoughts about the subject of feel.

We asked only a few questions, but received a lot of useful information. Golfers with a sound swing, low handicappers, and professionals remember the feel of their swing. They have taught themselves to repeat that feel or touch the next time they have the same type of shot. You have heard it referred to as Muscle Memory. Muscle Memory is feel.

"Because you can't see yourself swing a golf club, and feel alone is fickle, you can never know for sure whether you are actually doing what you think you are."

— Past U.S. Open Champion

Experienced golfers are not going over a specific "How to" on the golf course. Before the swing takes place, visualizations and feel are helping the golfer prepare for the swing. "How to" is important but only to a point. If the swing is going to be repeated, you must remember what the "How to" feels like to you.

Whether you make a good or bad swing, the INDIVIDUAL CHARACTERISTICS of what you are feeling as you swing must be remembered and recognized. Fast, Slow, Short, Long, Up, Down, etc. Everyone will feel their own swing a little differently, and it is this individual feel that is going to help you more than you can believe.

Learning is natural and learning is fun, or it should be. If you think you can learn, there is a good chance you will!

If your goal is to have a swing that can respond to what is called muscle memory, please accept that you should not be trying to memorize a lot of "How to." When the feel of the swing becomes more important than the "How to," PROGRESS is on the way.

We will spend time on the subject of feel later.

LET'S REVIEW:

- Progress will only come if you work!

- Progress is based (in part) on self-discovery!

- Suggestions you work with must be worthwhile!

- The body does not move on its own! REFLEXES — ANTICIPATION — MENTAL MESSAGES — create movement!

- Define the difference between "Personal Mannerisms of a golfer" are the movements and actions that exist in all sound swings!

- Concepts and Visualizations stored in your mind's eye are the most important keys in golf!

- We can be misled in golf by what we see and feel!

- Feel must become more important than thinking about "How to," if we are to make progress!

- Right side hemisphere of the brain is more helpful than Left side hemisphere.

UNDERSTANDING AND SEEING ANGULAR MOMENTUM, CENTRIFUGAL FORCE AND INERTIA AT WORK

An observation that most, if not all, in professional golf would agree on: "A sound swing creates centrifugal force, possesses inertia, and angular momentum."

Centrifugal Force, or center force, is the principle of force or power that is directed or created from a central point. It is a developing force, moving from the center outward.

Inertia is defined as matter, which if kept moving, will stay on the same path, unless affected by an outside force.

We believe very strongly, you will not have worthwhile golf concepts in your mind's eye unless you thoroughly understand and recall what centrifugal force and angular momentum are. The golf swing is founded on these laws and principles.

Good shots in golf are a result of a sound swing that has centrifugal force. Conversely, bad shots or swings occur only when there is no centrifugal force, or when centrifugal force is interrupted or stopped. Look at a sound swing or any efficient athletic movement and you are seeing centrifugal force, inertia and angular momentum at work.

Bobby Jones told us, "We use no more than the ordinary principles of motion that we encounter every day. Once the club starts on the correct path it will tend to hold its course until an outside force causes change." Alex Morrison said, "the swing starts from the center of the body under the influence of centrifugal force."

I do not know if you realize that power in golf and other sports comes from centrifugal force, or how you visualize it at work within the movements of the body during the sports you play or watch. So let's spend some time on the subject.

The expression we are going to use in explaining centrifugal force is *The Inside Moves the Outside*. These are what I feel are some key words from the definition of centrifugal force to keep in mind: INNER POINT, CENTRAL POINT, DEVELOPING, MOVES OUTWARD, KEEP MOVING, OUTSIDE FORCE.

- Power and energy from centrifugal force is a developing force, a force that builds up!
- Power and energy from centrifugal force moves outward from an inner or central point!
- Inertia will keep matter moving in the same direction, unless affected by an outside force!

We are spending time with detailed explanation of centrifugal force, so when it is referred to later, your mind's eye will have a worthwhile and clear concept of how a sound swing is under its influence when the inside is moving the outside.

Angular Momentum is the final factor we should have some knowledge about so we can better understand the workings of a sound golf swing.

Angular Momentum or the rotation of a mass around an axis is a subdivision of physics called Mechanics. When an object rotates around a fixed axis it will rotate at a constant rate of speed (until friction or gravity slows it down), so long as the objects total mass stays the same distance from the axis when rotating. When the objects mass is brought closer to the axis, it automatically speeds up, and if part of the object mass is moved further out from the axis the object slows down.

An example of this can be seen in the ice skater who is spinning at the center ice; the closer the arms of the skater are moved to the center or axis of the body mass, the faster the skater will spin. The further away the arms are moved from the skater's axis the slower the spin becomes.

The laws of motion and physics explain this result when science tells us; if the distribution of mass (or weight) with respect to the axis or center of the mass is changed, the rotational speed will change. Scientists also tell us the momentum or speed that has been created by rotation will generally move to the part of the system with the lesser mass, or part that is easiest to move.

When a long whip is snapped, the momentum travels away from the body mass, to the arm, to the hand, into the handle of the whip and out to the tip end of the whip. This tip has the least mass and therefore the easiest place for the momentum and speed to go. The tip end, in fact, travels so fast that when the whip "cracks" it is moving several hundred miles per hour.

When these three laws of physics are present in the swing, a golfer does not have to apply any conscious effort with his hands, arms, or club to produce a swing, it happens because of these laws of motion.

Angular Momentum, Centrifugal Force, and Inertia have each been explained separately. Now lets show or explain how they work with each other as a team.

When mass is in motion it has what is called *Inertia.* Inertia keeps a mass moving in a *straight line,* until affected by an outside force. The mass is also picking up "Velocity."

If the action that put a mass in motion is *circular* or *rotary*, Centrifugal Force will soon be present, and stay present as long as the circular motion exists.

Keep in mind, Inertia wants to keep matter moving in a *straight line*, at the same time the *circular* or *rotary* system is trying to move the mass in an *Arc*. Due to the fact that these two forces are working against each other, *Centrifugal Force is born*.

As the "Hub" (or center) of the system is turning in a circle, the *outer part* of the system that is trying to go in a straight line starts to *pull* against the hub. This pull is called Centrifugal Force, and it is what athletes "feel" when they are in motion.

Centrifugal Force is an outside force that interrupts Inertia, causing the outer part of the system to follow the lead of the hub and move in an arc or circle *instead of the straight line* inertia wants to move it in! Also, momentum and speed has traveled out to the tip end of the system because of Angular Momentum.

There are no straight lines in a sound golf swing. A sound golf swing moves in an arc. As you read on in the book, my hope for you is a true understanding of these two descriptions of the swing.

When the quality of the swing is less than we would like, it is because Centrifugal Force has been interrupted or stopped and the swing stops moving in an arc.

It's time to talk about the *"inside moving the outside."* Visualize a yard stick or put one down on a table. Now put your hand on the stick at the 3 inch mark. While keeping the bottom of the stick on the spot it started from, move the lower 3 inches of the stick left or right 3 inches. Note how much more the outside of the stick moves than the inside.

When the *inside moves the outside,* the outside will be moved a much greater distance. This fact of math and physics will be tied to your golf swing concepts shortly.

Another concept from math and physics that will help you to understand your golf swing is, when the inside moves slowly, the outside is moved much faster!

Visualize a skate line in an ice show. You can see the 20 to 30 girls start to move in a big circle. In a short time the outside girl is being moved at a greater speed and distance, while the inside girl is moving a very short distance and at a much slower speed. All the outside girl has to do is hold on. She could not move any faster or have more power if she tried to skate on her own. In fact, if she was to let go of the line and try to duplicate the speed and power that exist when holding on, we know she could not.

When a door closes, the inside of the door moves only inches and slowly, while the outside of the door moves many feet at a good pace.

With these visualizations in the mind's eye, you can start to build a sound swing. These are not only examples of the inside moving the outside, but they can be easily recognized. They can also answer questions about what makes a sound swing work.

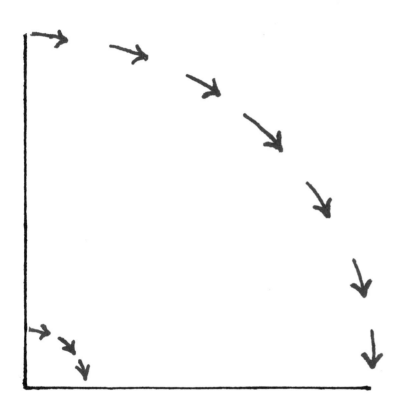

The inside moving the outside is leverage — wherein a small inside displacement causes a large outside displacement."

THE INSIDE MOVES THE OUTSIDE

In our golf instruction we ask people to label the ARMS, HANDS, and whatever is being held as the *"outside,"* and the rest of the body, FEET, LEGS, HIPS, CHEST, SHOULDERS and HEAD, the *"inside."*

We want people to have their *inside* move their *outside* when making a golf swing. To put it another way, we *do not* want a golfer to use their arms consciously during the swing. We feel when the arms are used, centrifugal force is either stopped or interrupted. When you consciously do nothing with the arms, they will follow the laws of physics and perform as they should in a sound swing.

Energy in golf or other sports is a result of a transfer of weight; you cannot transfer weight with your hands and arms *(or the outside)!* Weight will only be moved back and forth by your body *(or your inside).*

When asking you to see and to understand that the *inside* moves the *outside* in sports, I am also talking about the transfer of weight that is part of every efficient athletic movement that is under the influence of centrifugal force.

Your golf swing is very personal to you. At times it is very hard to get a golfer to change his mind on what he should be trying to do with his swing.

My hope for you is improvement. I believe that the arms do not have to do anything consciously in a sound swing. With the visualizations and concepts that will be shared with you, along with the statements from some very knowledgeable men, you may start to feel that *"The inside moves the outside."*

"Golf, while not an easy game, above all is a game of ease." Alex Morrison told us, and he went on, "You are probably saying, golf may be easy for you or some people, but it is hard for me. I have to concentrate or I'll miss the ball and I have to give it all I got or it won't ride. If there is such a thing as easy golf, there must be some formula for acquiring it. There has to be a positive method of overcoming my faults." There is a formula: "The Inside Moves the Outside."   (Mike Hebron)

Listed below are a few of the many statements I have come across over the years suggesting the same approach to the swing.

Ben Hogan: "The action of the arms is motivated by the movements of the body, and the hands consciously do nothing but maintain a firm grip on the club."

Bobby Jones: "The proper order of movement is body, then arms, and last the club head."

Alex Morrison: The swing starts from the center of the body, under the influence of centrifugal force."

Paul Runyan: "The swing is entirely controlled by the shifting and turning of body weight. The arms become a connecting link, and nothing more, between the pivot point and the club head."

Ben Hogan: "The main thing for the average golfer is to keep any conscious hand action out of his swing. The correct swing is founded on a chain action. If you use the hands when you should not, you prevent the chain action."

Paul Runyan: "It is my experience that as you 'cease' consciously directing the swing by the use of shoulders and arm muscles, you establish an automatic grooved swing."

Carl Lohren: "Whenever the arms and hands are involved in your mental concept, they will steal the show. If the hands and arms move first, they will not direct the club in the proper direction."

Ben Hogan: "Next time you see a good player in action, note how his body appears to drive forward before he hits the ball."

Paul Runyan: "Do not try to uncock or snap your wrists. This is an automatic motion caused by the natural flow of the club head as maximum speed is attained."

Ben Hogan: "To start the downswing, forget about the shoulders, arms and hands."

Carl Lohren: "As you start, exert no influence on the club with the hands and arms. Do not be afraid that they will not go where they are supposed to go."

Paul Runyan: "Note the club is not lifted back, but the initial movement in the backswing of shifting and turning results in the club moving back."

Tom Watson, Jack Nicklaus, and Alex Morrison talked in length about the hands and arms playing a less important role in the swing than they had originally visualized.

Alex told us, "I have been convinced. A careful study of the technique of every expert who has played in the United States, proves conclusively that every successful shot played by any one of them is the direct result of the employment of centrifugal force. Despite *everything I had heard*, I could not make myself believe that the main force of a golf swing should originate in the hands and arms. Trial and experiment demonstrated to me that the necessary whirling motion of the club was produced only when the force activating the club had its origin near the center of the body."

"Moreover, Bobby Jones' swing illustrates this motion better than the swing of any other golfer. In other words, the sound swing is not my swing, nor Jones, nor Smith, but simply the exemplification of a scientific principle correctly applied."

"My definition of the swing is 'One full smooth flowing motion without any mental or physical interruption'. Only by winding up the body to its fullest, then releasing the accumulated force in any expanding motion, can a golf club be swung easily, naturally, accurately, and with maximum power."

Jack Nicklaus, since the spring of 1980, has changed his beliefs about the golf swing. His swing was always marked by his high flying arms. He now feels some of what he wrote or said in clinics in the past is incorrect and contrary to how he tries to swing today. (He has lost POWER with his old swing).

Jack, knowing golf is always a learning process, said with apologies, "I decided to find a new and better swing. If the arms are over extended early in the backswing, it is a lazy, lift up, chop way to play — extremely common among recreational golfers. My challenge was to flatten my swing, so I began hugging the upper chest with my arms in the backswing."

In the past, Jack's arms (his outside) were moving on their own early in his backswing and this would stop the coil that helps create power in the swing. You see, the less you turn your upper body going back, the less tension or coil you can create to be used in the form of centrifugal force in the front swing.

The smaller the upper body or coil going back, the slower the club head will be moving on the way forward. This is due to the loss of centrifugal force and angular momentum that can be created in the front swing when the backswing turn is completed.

When golfers use their arms to make their backswing they often do not complete the turn going back. This happens because the arms have gone up or back on their own, causing a false sense of a full backswing. This lack of a completed backswing results in a lack of coil that creates Centrifugal Force and Angular Momentum.

Tom Watson told us, "I became a consistent driver only this year (1982). In the past I would make a false turn because my hands started first, shoulders not turning enough — now I start everything away from the ball together. Arms close to body — now my swing is more efficient, arms and body in harmony."

Tom also said, "On the course I'm reminding myself to have my arms closer to my body." The thoughts from Tom Watson and Jack Nicklaus were found in *Golf Digest* articles.

The week before Jack Nicklaus won.the 1986 Masters, the April 6 headline in the Augusta Chronical said, "Nicklaus takes game to lesson tee."

The story told its readers that Nicklaus was on the practice range making a few swing corrections that he hoped would improve what he called "Horrendous play this year."

"Basically I've taken the hands out of my game," said Nicklaus. "I was playing with too much hands. I still want to win and think I can," and he did!

"Old"

"New"

Jack Nicklaus

"I was lifting out of my plane on just about every backswing I made."

— Jack Nicklaus

From *Medicine and Sports, Vol. 2,* came the following viewpoint. "With electronic testing of the muscles and high speed, motion picture analysis, it was found that average players, when compared to top-ranked players, fail to use momentum of the trunk and end up relying mostly on the arms resulting also in not having as late or as rapid a release."

In 1946, Percy Boomer wrote, "From the shoulders, our power travels down through the arms, and as to arm action, I also believe the following common conception to be erroneous. Most people think they lift their arms to get them to the top of the back swing. With a modern controlled swing (Modern in 1946), they do not lift — the arms work absolutely subjectively to the shoulders. That is why they are controlled. The triangle formed by our arms and the line between the shoulders should never lose its shape. It should be possible to push a wooden snooker triangle in between the arms and leave it there without impeding the swing, back or through. The arms have not been lifted; they have gone up in response to the shoulder movement."

These are the basic movements of a connected and therefore, controlled swing, and they must all be built into the framework of your feel of the swing."

One of today's well-known teachers, Jim Ballard, talks about the triangle and its connection in his recent book.

Percy went on to say, "If you keep these three basic feels; the pivot, the shoulders moving in response to the pivot and the arms moving in response to the shoulders, nothing much will go wrong with your game."

"So, we never have to consciously produce a good shot. We have to merely make certain movements which we have been taught and which will result in a good shot." He was talking about trusting your swing, and you can trust it if the "inside is moving the outside."

Byron Nelson, when talking about the discoveries that helped his game, (I believe) made some comments that you will find interesting and helpful.

He talked about seeing pictures of leading amateur and professional golfers of his day "Rolling their wrists" as the swing nears the ball — as a result of a series of experiments, he found that when he did not try to roll his wrists, and just let them stay in place for "about thirty inches before impact and through the early stages of the follow through," he increased his accuracy.

Byron also talked about the best way to insure a well-timed swing. He felt that one should start the backswing in a single motion, shoulders, hands and clubhead together.

Here is the triangle at address Percy Boomer is talking about. On page 28 you can see this triangle during the full swing.

"I learned to play golf with my legs and torso. My hands and wrists involuntarily did their job just fine when everything else (legs and torso) worked properly."
— Past British Open Champion

Byron stopped trying to add extra movements to his hands (outside).

You have just read some thoughts from the leaders in the world of golf, on how the hands and arms should not be separated from your body. If they are, they may stop your game from reaching the level it is capable of.

Remember, we would like your swing to be founded on the principles of Centrifugal Force, to have your *outside* (hands, arms and club) moved by a transfer of weight created by your *inside* (legs and upper body). Angular Momentum, Inertia, Centrifugal Force and Kinetic Energy can help you create a sound swing automatically.

The Triangle during the full swing.

SEE THE SWING AS A WHEEL

It may be helpful to visualize the swing as a wheel with spokes. This can give you a little more understanding on how a golf swing works, and where power and energy come from when the swing is in motion. Picture the *club head* as the outermost part of a wheel, the "rim." Next, picture the *shaft* of the club and your *hands and arms* as the "spokes" of this wheel. The "HUB" or center of the wheel is your *spine*.

Science tells us the most efficient way to start a wheel in motion that is going to stay on its axis would be to apply FORCE to its center or "HUB." This *Force* then travels out or is transmitted centrifugally through the spokes to the outtermost part of the wheel automatically.

One of our goals in golf should be to make the most efficient swing possible, and repeat this swing as often as we can automatically. A swing can be repeated if the "hub" of the swing does not change positions when the swing is in motion. Another way of saying this — we want the "hub" of the swing to revolve on its axis throughout the back and forth motion of the swing.

The best way to keep the swing on its axis when it is in motion, or prevent the "hub" of the swing from changing positions, would be to start your "hub" or center of the swing moving first. (The same as starting a wheel from its hub).

If you were to start your swing from either your hands, forearms, or upper arms, the swing would not start by first causing its "hub" to revolve. Instead, the joint just above the part used bends. Moving the hands first could cause a wrist break or roll. Using the forearms could cause a bend at the elbow very early in the backswing. Both movements leave the swing without extension or width. Letting the upper arms start the swing could cause the shoulder joint to become the "hub" or center.

Your goal is to have a swing that can repeat, and it will repeat when it stays on its axis. When the first move in the swing comes from its center it will stay on its axis The laws of physics and motion will help create a sound swing with power, without any conscious use of your hands and arms when the *Inside Moves the Outside.*

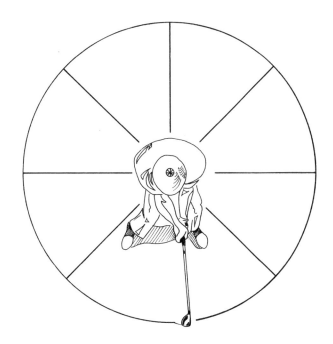

SEE IT WORK IN OTHER SPORTS

Before moving on to the golf swing, let's examine how the *inside moves the outside* in other popular and easy to recognize athletic movements. Your visualization should improve after this section.

Picture a major league third baseman having a ground ball hit to him. He picks it up and makes a good throw to first base and the batter is out.

Now, let's take a closer look at what he did with his body. As he bends down to field the ball, his chest, hips and shoulders are all facing the ball (Pictures A). As the ball is picked up, his arms do not move, but his shoulders, chest, hips, and legs (*inside*) turn away from first base, and his arm (*outside*) and ball are moved behind him. *The inside has moved the outside* (Pictures B).

Can you imagine the infielder just moving his arm to make a throw — (without turning his body)? Not only would it look "hurky jerky," but the throw would have no power. This occurs because when the (*outside*) arm moves on its own, there is no centrifugal force built up.

As the first baseman awaits the ball. he will first see the infielder's (*inside*) legs, then the hips, then the chest, and finally, the (*outside*) arm move under the influence of centrifugal force. (Pictures C).

Note how much faster his arm (*outside*) was moving than his body (*inside*). While the body made a somewhat smallish turn, look how far the hand (*outside*) traveled. The arms and chest stayed almost in the same position relative to one another during most of the throwing motion. You do not get the impression that the arm (*outside*) took off on its own at any time. It almost held the same position it was in when the ball was first picked up, in relation to the chest.

Remember, if an athletic movement is under the influence of Centrifugal Force the outside will be moved very fast even though the inside is moving much slower.

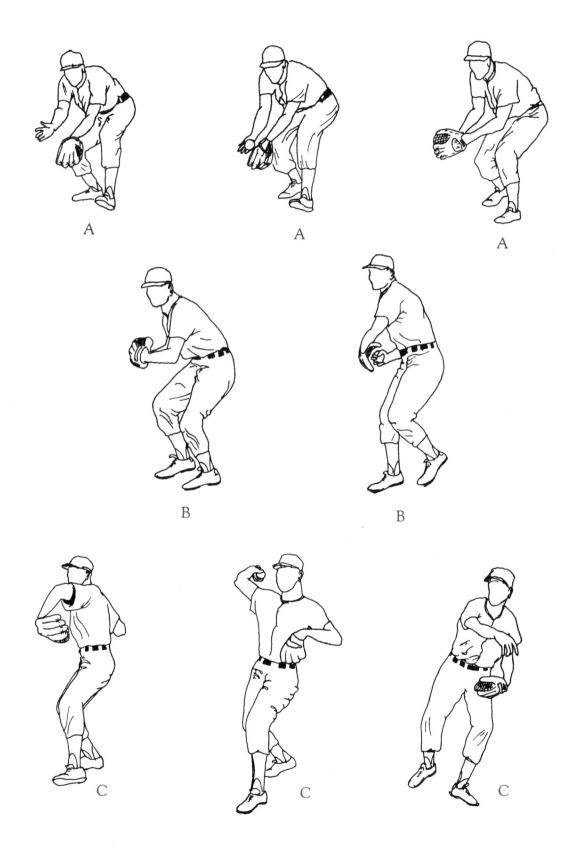

A   A   A

B   B

C   C   C

When watching a big league pitcher, you also can see the body (inside) moving much slower than his arm (outside). Note how much his body (inside) is turned to the left of home plate after the pitch is delivered. If at any point in the attempt to move the ball forward, the body (inside) was to stop, and the (outside) arm was to try and finish the action, the body (inside) would not be in that easy to recognize finished position. The body must keep turning forward if the arm is to have any speed or power, and it must also turn to the position where the right side is closer to home plate than the left side.

A sound, finished golf swing will have the right side closer to the target than the left. Ben Hogan told us how he wanted the swing to finish with the right side closer to the target. "At the completion of the swing, the player's belt buckle does not point directly at his target. It should definitely point to the left of his target."

When the quarterback is about to receive the ball, his shoulders, chest, legs, and feet all are facing downfield. As he takes the ball and steps back, the hands, arms and ball are in the same position they were in when he first took the ball. Then the upper body (inside) *starts to turn the arms and ball back.* You can see the chest and shoulders turn away from downfield, carrying the arm and ball back (outside). Then when he wants the ball to go forward, his lower body steps forward. The left leg and the hips unwind (coaches want the quarterbacks to work on turning their hip to throw the ball). This is followed by the chest, shoulders, and finally, the last part of the body the defense will see is the (outside) arm and ball brought forward into the throwing position.

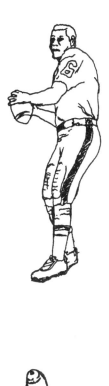 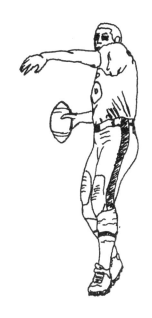 

During the ground strokes, a tennis coach wants the racket brought back by the turning of the (inside) chest and shoulders. When it is time to serve, if we were to stand directly in front of the player serving, we could see the body, the (inside) legs, hips, chest, and shoulders turn forward, and finally, in the trailing position, the arm and racket are brought forward.

Imagine the arm and racket going forward without the body moving first. It would be an awful serve.

When a batter's baseball swing starts forward, we can see the lower body (inside) being led by the legs. Then the hips start to turn forward, followed by the chest, the shoulders, and last, as in all other athletic motions under the influence of centrifugal force, the arms, hands, and bat.

This is how a sound golf swing works. The less you use your hands and arms consistently, the more progress your game will make. The arms and hands are being moved. They are moved under the influence of centrifugal force, that creates a load factor that in turn breaks your wrists going back and again in the forward swing with the stored up power being released.

THE GOLF SWING IN MOTION

Before a swing can be considered sound, it must have what I call some pre-requisites.

1. The upper body starts the swing back, and the lower body starts it forward.

2. The swing must have width and extension, with the club head traveling in the widest arc.

3. The club must move on a path or plane that is constant and can be repeated.

4. The backswing must create torque, wind up, or coil, in the lower back that is going to help bring the swing forward and expand the arms and club on the target line.

5. The swing must transfer weight back and forth. Energy and power in sports is a transfer of weight. (You cannot transfer any weight with the 'outside' arms and hands.)

6. The angle that is caused when the wrist breaks at the top of the backswing must be held during the forward swing. (Retain the angle.)

7. The swing should finish with the right side closer to the target than the left, and the body must feel spent.

8. The golfer should have the feeling that he/she stays at the same height throughout the swing.

9. The arms should feel light and relaxed in the swing.

10. A golfer should feel like the club is the last thing to move, or that it has been left behind as the swing goes forward.

The golf swing's assignment is to move the club on a path that has a relationship to a target.

The golfer's responsibility is to develop a simple system that can meet this assignment.

Getting the swing in motion (or the backswing) in our view, starts from above the waist, without the use of the hands and arms. When you are standing to the ball correctly (we will cover this later), all we want you to do is to start your upper body back. Because all golfers will not feel the swing in the same way, your concept of how to do this may be different from your neighbor's. If we were to take pictures of several golfers, all making a good or sound backswing, there would be a good chance all would have a different key to make the back move. The important point is not to do anything with your hands or arms. You may want to start by turning your back to the target, or have the feeling of turning your chest over your right foot. Someone else may turn their right shoulder around their neck. (Arnold Palmer used this thought at one time.) Some golfers picture a triangle made up of the shoulders and two arms, and they just turn this triangle back with the upper body, or the suggestion Carl Lohren uses, start the swing with the left shoulder area.

In my view, because we play golf with our nervous system, there has to be some personal discovery to find the best visualization for the start of your backswing. Just do not use your arms or hands, or have the feeling you are either going up or down with your body, and make sure there is a weight transfer.

Picture your chest as a mirror and the club head would be reflected in that mirror for most of the backswing.

THE BACKSWING IS ONLY INCHES LONG

Now if you have started your swing without the arms, and the (*inside*) upper body has done its job, and you are in the full coil position with the back facing the target, YOU HAVE ONLY MOVED A FEW INCHES, not several feet! Look at where the left shoulder started in the swing and the spot it stops at the end of the coil. It has only moved inches. The backswing is only a few inches long, no longer.

D.S. Meyer, in his book, showed that in the full golf swing, the club head covers about 27 feet, takes about 2 seconds, with the speed of the head reaching 80 to 100 mph.

He is talking about the club head moving 27 feet, remember the club head is part of the *outside*. When you move your (*inside*) upper body inches on the backswing, the club head travels many times that amount due to the laws of math and physics (remember our example of using the yardstick).

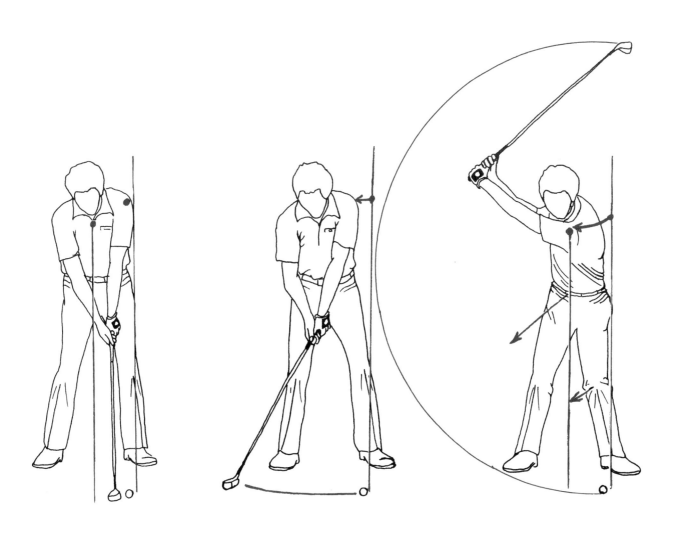

While the club head outside has traveled a great distance, the inside has only moved a few inches.

If your visualization and concepts have been larger or bigger than inches, you are making your backswing more complicated than it has to be. Picture the backswing as small or short, and the club will go to the finish of your backswing because of the laws of math and physics. The end of the backswing should be visualized as a spot most golfers feel is the halfway point of the backswing.

The reason the club goes to the position we normally picture or call the finish of the backswing is because of momentum and the load factor, not because we swing it there.

When the *inside* is turning the *outside*, the club head is being moved under the influence of centrifugal force and is picking up speed, momentum and weight. When the club head reaches what we would normally call halfway back, with our coil or turn completed, the club head (*outside*) keeps going back because of momentum, and the load factor causes the club to cock the wrists. The arms have done nothing. The hands have done nothing. For most of the backswing the arms have moved because the inside moved them, but in the final stage of the backswing, the arms and hands are moving into the top backswing position because of momentum and load factor. You don't try to control this move. You try to control the size of your coil, not control what the arms and hands are doing. Let them do their thing. Let them feel free of control.

Example: When looking at a skate line going around and around, if the inside girl on the line was suddenly to stop, would the outside girl stop at the same time? No! She would keep moving for a short time. This is because of momentum and load factor. The same action occurs in a sound golf swing.

Also, as you finish your wind up, (which we now should be visualizing as only a few inches) one of the results of the backswing is that under the momentum and load factor, the lower body starts forward before the club stops going back.

We said that most golfers we have seen have a backswing that is too long. You should now have some understanding of why this happens. When you try to swing the club all the way back to the spot we traditionally have accepted as the top or end of the backswing, the club will travel beyond that point because of the laws of physics and momentum. The overswing is caused by poor visualization of the backswing compounded by the hands and arms bringing the club back, rather than the *inside* Remember, the backswing is only a few inches long!

"My wrists hinge reflexively in response to the swing momentum of the club head."
— Past PGA Champion

When you see pictures of Hogan's swing, you can see his lower body move forward before the backswing seems to be completed. But we now know that the backswing is over long before the arms and club stop going backwards. You can see this happen in all sound swings.

During the throwing action of several sports (baseball, bowling, etc.) the hand and arm is still moving back as you are stepping forward.

Here is an illustration of what happens in a sound swing. When you try to swing to position A - the club - hands and arms will travel to position B automatically when the inside is moving the outside.

A   B

Here are illustrations of Janet Coles taken from pictures I had taken. Picture A is where you should be trying to make your swing travel to, but the position in Picture B is where your swing will go to when it is under the influence of momentum and load factor. Picture your backswing as small or short and the laws of math and physics will put the club in the normally accepted position.

The backswing can only lose its width and extension if you try to do something with your hands or arms on the way back. (This would be similar to the *outside* girl on the skate line letting go and going off on her own.) Trust just letting the arms move because of your upper body turn. Also, having the feeling that your upper arms are staying on your chest during the backswing will help your swing.

I have asked golfers to feel like their upper arms are surgically sewn to their chests and to leave them there. In a sound swing, the arms stay on the chest. If they do leave this position, it is only slightly and only for a moment. But preferably, both arms should feel like they are close to the chest in the backswing with the left arm *never* moving off the chest at any time during the backswing.

When the upper body (*inside*) creates the backswing, the club will stay on its proper path or plane. This is the line or path the club must travel every time if we are to have a swing that will repeat and can be trusted.

SWING PATH OR PLANE

A sound golf swing will stay on plane when in motion. At address, your arms are extended at an angle. The degree of this angle depends on the size and posture of the golfer. A tall golfer will have a more perpendicular or upright angle. Our shorter golfer will have a flatter or more acute angle. The posture or set up causes what plane or path your swing will have. If you were to see a golfer making a shot where the ball was waist high, (off a side hill lie, or stuck in a bush or tree), you would see a swing that would go back and forth or around the spine (the golfer's spine is perpendicular to the ground during this type of shot).

When looking at the same golfer making a swing with the ball on the ground, we *may* picture the swing as going up and down. In my view, this would be very harmful. The swing should be pictured as back and forth from the target, not up and down from the ball.

When the golfer hits a ball on the ground his spine tilts over, giving the impression that the club is going up. Actually, the club is traveling on the same path to the spine, as when the golfer was standing straight up for the waist high shot — back and forth or around. The person who feels the club has gone up is being misled by what he sees because the club is traveling, or should be, on a path around the spine, and the degree of tilt in the spine causes the shape of the swing that our eyes see. Swings with long clubs will look more around than swings with short clubs. The more we tilt or bend over, the more up the swing will look. But the sound swing is always on plane moving in an arc around the spine. Do not be misled.

Picturing your shoulders turning around your spine can be helpful. Never picture up or down.

We ask golfers to picture the "Hogan Visualization" of the plate glass that sits across his shoulders at the angle that is caused by his posture. This plate of glass defines the path of Hogan's swing plane. When he made his swing it traveled just under the glass. So will yours if you do nothing with your hands and arms.

By just turning your upper body, the club travels on your plane automatically. It can only go on this path because it is under the influence of centrifugal force and momentum. The main cause of a swing moving off its plane is that the arms make an extra move in the backswing. When starting the backswing, do not go up or down with your body or arms.

If the *outside* (hands and arms) does nothing but lets itself be turned by the upper body (*inside*), the club will stay on your swing plane because "Matter once moving, if kept moving, will stay on its path, unless affected by an outside force."

When a golfer sets up correctly (bending from the hips, tilting the spine, flexing the knees, buttocks out, head off the chest) and stays in this posture throughout the swing, it will help keep the swing on plane or in the correct path.

At the top of the backswing, if your left wrist is in a straight line with the back of the left hand, and the face of the club is square, and the shaft is PARALLEL to both the ground and target line, THE CLUB IS ON PLANE.

If the shaft of the club is parallel to the target line as the swing gets waist high in both the front and back swing, THE CLUB IS ON PLANE.

If the grip end of the club points at the target line when the swing is between waist high and the top of the swing, THE CLUB IS ON PLANE.

When a golfer lets his hands, arms, and club respond to "the inside" or "hub," there is an in plane roll of the left arm.

The left wrist, at address, is facing straight towards the target and exactly along the plane of aim, but at the top of the backswing, it ends up lying flat within the plane, and facing 90° to the target line. (Left palm "down," right palm "up.")

Research tells us: It seems certain that the key in getting to the correct top-of-back-swing position is the first foot or so of the backswing. If this is correct, the rest of the backswing will tend to follow naturally. This is why professionals so often advise a "one-piece takeaway."

The versatile joint of the left shoulder tends to roll the arm. This 30° roll of the left arm is natural or automatic, unless the golfer INTERFERES.

Short

Tall

"I stand tall, then stay tall. I maintain my weight in the hips, shoulders, and head throughout the swing."

— Past T.P.C. Champion

The movements happen quite naturally if they are given the chance to. The simple in-plane roll and cocking of the wrist is merely the natural conclusion, caused by the backswing momentum of the club and the way the left shoulder joint works.

The clubhead also follows the whole "hub" action during the early stages of the downswing and forwardswing. It will be the "hub" action which sets the plane pattern and timing of the swing forward. (Not hands and arms.)

During the frontswing the wrist is not only uncocking, but is also rotating along with the left forearm back on its own axis. As with the backswing, the roll happens automatically because of the in-plane momentum of the clubhead.

Even when power is added by wrist action, whether uncocking or rolling, it is merely as a *help* to the natural outswinging action of the clubhead that had its origin at the "hub" of the swing. (This has been validated by research.)

A full coil of the upper body will be created when the upper body (*inside*) is given the responsibility of creating the backswing. A full coil must occur before the swing starts forward. There are two common ways of preventing coil. First, the over use of the lower body in the backswing. The lower body must move a shorter distance than the upper body if you are going to create the tension in the muscles of the lower back that gives some of the energy the forward swing needs. It should feel as though you are moving your upper body against the lower body similar to winding up a child's toy. If the toy was to move in the same direction or distance as the key you are turning, the toy's spring would not wind up.

We like to tell golfers to almost try to keep the lower body out of the backswing, and the turn of the upper body will naturally pull the lower body into the action of the backswing just enough. When throwing a ball a short distance, our legs and hips would be moved a very short distance. If the throw was a longer one, the legs and hips are moved a larger distance. This happens because of the bigger upper body coil caused by wanting to throw the ball a longer distance.

Muscles of the lower back are attached to the hip area of the body and will pull the lower body into the backswing. It is very natural to let the lower body follow the upper body going backwards in sports. So, let's use the same system for your golf swing. Don't think very much about your lower body and it will be moved the correct amount during the coil back.

A visualization that has helped many golfers is to have the feeling that the right leg does not move in the backswing. It may move a small amount but the movement will stay to a mini-

Over use of the lower body can cause the center of gravity to move past our base of support.

Upper body has moved more than the lower and the right leg has stayed in place.

mum by trying not to move the leg at all. Also, as a result of a proper coil, the left knee will point back past the ball. (Illustrations on page 51.)

Another good visualization is that "golf is played inside the feet." In the backswing, your body or the weight that is going backwards should not go outside your right foot. The same is true for the front swing, during this part of the swing, your body should not pass your left foot. Play golf inside your feet. When trying to keep the right leg in place, the swing will stay inside the right foot nicely. The head will also turn or release slightly during the backswing. If the head does not turn, it makes it almost impossible to have any weight move back on the right side. The movement is very small, but it should be part of the backswing.

I also like to have golfers keep their weight more to the heels during the backswing. Try this exercise and you will see why. Put your body in the position where you are about to throw a ball forward. Your upper body is turned away from your target, with your arm back. At this point your weight will be on your right heel. Hold that position and move the weight off your right heel to your right toe. You will start to lose your balance. Now put the weight back on your heel. You are now back in a balanced and powerful position to move forward.

The second way of destroying a good coil is to have your arms (*outside*) move on their own anywhere in the backswing. This is what Jack Nicklaus and Tom Watson found happening to their swings a few years ago. Their coil was not what they were looking for. With the arms taking over the backswing, the arms would try to finish the backswing. Both told us that the body would stop turning because of a false sense of having made a completed backswing when the arms got to the top on their own.

Your backswing will have coil, width, extension, and stay in its plane when you do nothing with your arms (*outside*) and just let them be moved back by the upper body (*inside*). Also, please remember to picture the backswing as inches in size, not several feet.

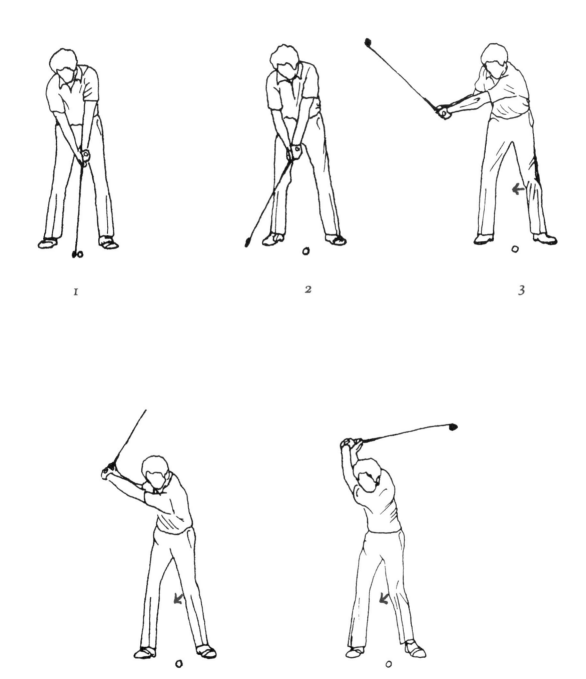

1

2

3

4

5

Note how the right leg does not move very much in a sound backswing, and the left knee is pointing back past the ball.

PLANE VISUALIZATION

When the swing is on plane the right palm faces up and the left palm faces down.

OFF PLANE

FULL SWING VISUALIZATION

Here is a picture of the full swing. It is the kind of picture that most golfers would use as a model of what positions a sound swing goes through. All of the easy to recognize positions, (hands, arms, and club) can be seen.

It is my view that golfers will only confuse themselves, or make progress with their swing harder than it has to be, if they are concerned with what the hands, arms and club are doing in the swing.

This is a drawing of Ben Hogan, but a picture of any swing can give the impression the golf swing is large. But in my view, the swing is very small, when the *inside* is moving the *outside*.

There is no need to have a picture of the swing in your mind that is a big one. You should only be concerned with a turn, and what the body does to accomplish the movement of weight, not what the hands and arms are doing.

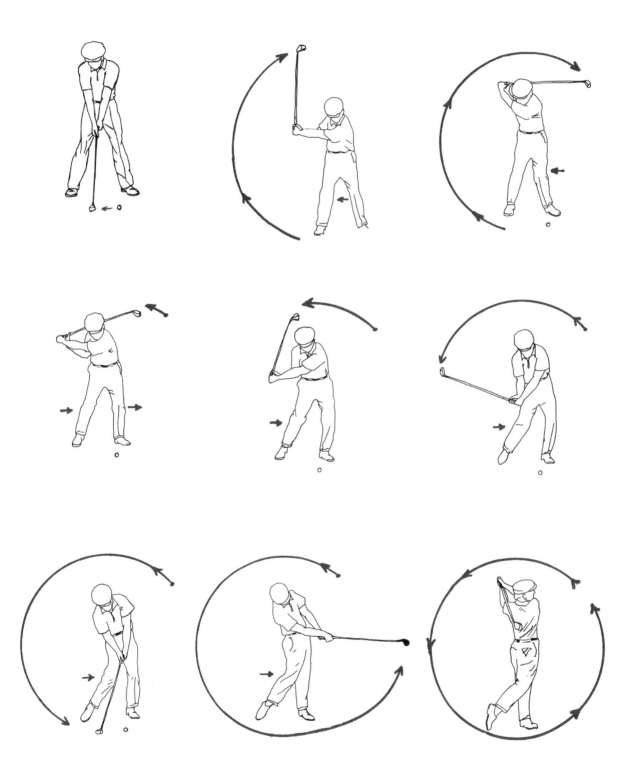

VISUALIZING THE SWING WITHOUT THE HANDS, ARMS AND CLUB

We are now showing Ben Hogan's swing without the hands, arms and club. You can see how small the golf swing really is, when the hands, arms and club are not part of your visualization.

The swing is only inches back and inches forward. The upper body is going back with the lower body starting the swing forward.

It is not necessary to have a picture of the hands, arms and club in your mind, or try and do anything with them during the swing. It will be more helpful to be able to recognize what the body or inside must do in the swing.

Recognize how small the golf swing is. The hands, arms and club (*outside*) are moved (as a unit) a great distance by the body (*inside*) that has moved only inches while creating centrifugal force.

EVEN IN THE SAND, THE INSIDE
MOVES THE OUTSIDE

For most people who play golf, the sand shot has always been thought of as a hand and arm swing, but when you see pictures of a good sand player you can see the hands and arms being moved as a unit by the *"Inside."*

The unit of the hands and arms can be pictured as a triangle — and it does not travel on its own during the swing. Notice how the upper arms stay on the chest throughout the swing as the *"Inside"* moves the *"Outside."*

Because the sand shot, at times, requires a lot of height, there is sometimes a small wrist break at the start, for extra height. This does not always (wrist break) start the sand shot.

Forget the arms and let the *Inside move the Outside!*

LEAVE THE CLUB BEHIND

It can be seen in all sports and golf is no exception. *The inside moves the outside.* Many take up golf because it looks like fun and not all that hard to learn. If you have been playing golf for a while, it may not be easy for you to accept such a simple thought. You may have worked very hard to make progress using tips and suggestions that were not as simple. If you have played some good golf, the following statement you may find hard to accept. You do not have to think about your arms or putting the club here or there.

Trust me, the arms, hands, and club will go to the correct positions when the inside moves the outside. The laws of math and physics are on your side. These laws cause the correct position as a direct result of doing nothing with the hands and arms.

This is how a blind golfer is able to play. The club finds the ball because it is kept in its plane under the influence that was created by centrifugal force. When you do not alter the path the club wants to take (*with the inside moving the outside*) you will hit very powerful and straight shots, and you will feel very much at ease during the swing.

Of all the statements that will be shared with you, there is one that may give the most understanding to what happens in the sound golf swing. Bobby Jones said, "The all important feel which I experience as the swing changes direction is that I have the distinct feeling that I have left the club behind as I start forward." Go back and read what Mr. Jones said again.

Look at any athlete in motion, and you can see the arm, hands, and whatever else is being held has been left behind as the rest of the body starts forward.

The baseball pitcher, the batter, the quarterback, the tennis player, the infielder, all look as though the arm has been left behind as the body starts forward. As the inside moves forward, the outside is finally brought to its speed and full power after being left behind.

When looking at the sound swing, it too looks like the arm and club have been left behind. It looks this way because that is what is happening. In the sound swing, the body starts forward and the arms do not move on their own. They are not pulling down. They are, if you like, pulled forward. To some it may feel like the arm is pulling because of the power that has been built up by the *inside* bringing them forward.

Use this as a swing key. Try to leave your arms behind when you start your front swing. They will come forward at the correct time, not before, when you try your best to keep them out of the swing.

If the arms were to pull, this would be like the *outside* girl on the skate line letting go of the line and trying to skate by herself. If the motion of centrifugal force in the golf swing is interrupted, all the energy of this natural power would be lost. You are left only with momentum, and that would soon be lost or continued artifically by the hands (*outside*) trying to hit.

Let's visualize how the body moves in all sports. The upper body (above the waist) always starts the movement back, and the lower body always initiates the movement forward.

Years ago, trying to give golfers a simple concept to play with I said, "turn your back to the target going back, use your legs going forward, and finish with the weight on the front foot" with no mention of the arms.

This was the suggestion that a lot of very successful golfers built their swing on.

Watching the arms and club in the swing of a good player, I feel, is not as helpful to your visualization as looking at the movements of the body and how the body moves the arms and club. Over the years, I have found that when golfers try to leave the club behind, several important and required results in the swing are taken care of automatically.

One important result: the right shoulder is lowered and the plane of the swing becomes slightly flatter and more from the inside. The club is now approaching the ball from inside the target line and will produce a square club face at impact. This happens without any use of the hands because the golfer has let the lower body lead the forward swing and has left the hands and club behind.

Also, the inside path of the clubhead assures that the bodies leverage and force will be behind the hit, giving your swing the ability to generate maximum power. (To move an object forward you must be in back of it.)

The change of direction from back to front happens slowly in a sound swing. A good swing key is to try and change direction slowly.

Do not try and roll your hands. They are moved as a unit by the inside. Sometimes it looks like they roll, but that is because of the angle you are looking from, and you are being misled by what you think you see.

(Explanation on page 103-114)

Position A is the top or finish of the backswing. In position B you can clearly see the body has moved forward while the (outside) hands, arms and club have been left behind.

LAG - DRAG - PRESSURE - NO SLACK

Lag, Drag, Pressure, and No Slack are other conditions that exist in all sound golf swings when a golfer leaves the club behind as he goes forward (avoiding any conscious use of the hands and arms).

For *no slack* to be present in a swing, the lower body will have to start forward before the club has finished going back, and this does happen in a sound swing. This move starts the swing forward in a tight sequence, preventing any slack from entering the swing.

When the lower body starts forward, and the club shaft is still going back, this causes two other needed conditions to occur. First, this lower body movement forward helps add to the wrist flex that happens in the backswing: it also puts *DOWN PRESSURE* on the club's shaft that can now be transferred as *PRESSURE* on the ball as it is hit.

A sound swing always puts pressure on the ball, compressing it onto the clubface. This pressure comes from the *down pressure* that started to LOAD UP the shaft in the first stage of the front swing.

This same kind of pressure can be seen building up in a "fly rod" shaft as the handle of the rod changes directions to move the hook and line forward into the water.

When the wrists are fully flexed and the club's shaft has the needed pressure on it, now all the sound swing has to do is drag the clubhead forward. The sound swing leaves the club behind and the laws of motion bring it forward at the expected and correct time, giving the feeling of "lagging" and "dragging" the club.

Down pressure causes the shaft to flex down in the front swing, (when the inside is moving the outside). This pressure is then applied to the ball.

  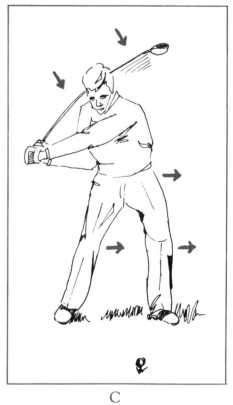

A   B   C

RETAIN THE ANGLE

In Hogan's swing, there are two positions I would like to point out. One is of the master at the top of his swing, and the other is his swing as it moves into the hitting area of the swing. In picture A, the hands and arms are back. In picture B, they are about to unload all the power of the swing through the ball. The hand, arms and club have moved a good distance, but as Hogan tells us, he has done nothing with the arms. In fact, he said to forget them when making your swing. (He has moved his *inside*.)

This is an example of pure *inside moving the outside*. The club has traveled several feet, while the body has moved only a short distance.

"Retain the Angle," "Retain the Angle" some books and golf teachers will loudly suggest. During the front swing, they want golfers not to change the angle or position that the hands and wrists fall into at the top of the backswing until the impact area. In my view, when you do nothing consciously with the hands, arms, and club in the front swing, this all important move of retaining the angle is automatically accomplished. It has to be. The only time the angle will break down is when the golfer tries to do something with the swing besides moving forward with the lower inside.

This position that the hands, arms, and club fall into at the top does not change until the centrifugal force and angular momentum that is influencing the swing causes the clubhead to expand the wrist and arms and whack the hell out of the ball. The centrifugal force that we are talking about is created by the *inside body moving the outside body*.

Also, the *inside* is moving the swing forward. In picture B - if it was a child's plastic toy that could be moved into different positions - and you put your fingers on the golfer's shoulder and turned them back to the point they were in for picture A - you can clearly see the hands, arms and club stay in the same position for both pictures.

The hands, arms and club have been moved as a unit by the *inside*. They have not moved on their own.

Note that the hands are the   distance from the shoulder in both pictures, and you will also find the angle of the wrists has not changed in either picture.

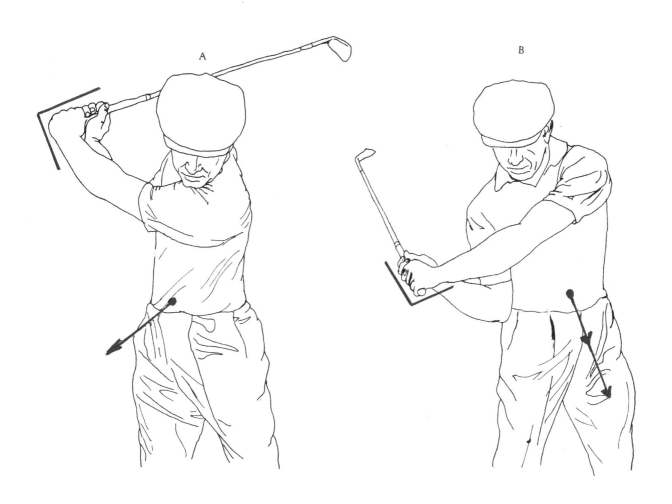

When the hands and arms do nothing, and are moved by the inside, the ANGLE is retained.

The position the club, hands and arms fall into at the top of the swing will not change in a sound swing until angular momentum and centrifugal force expands them.

Also, because of the expanding power of centrifugal force at the point of ball contact in a good swing, the arms have been expanded, fully stretched out (they come to a relaxed and spent position behind the body at the end of the swing).

After ball contact, the clubhead has all the energy of the swing. This happens because of the power created by angular momentum and centrifugal force that moves outward and into the clubhead from the body. Because of this, you should have the feeling that the clubhead is now pulling you around to the finished balanced position, with body feeling relaxed and spent with most of your weight on the front foot. Do not force the finish; let it happen as a result of doing nothing consciously with the *outside*, and the *inside* creating centrifugal force will cause the finish of your swing.

Some golf instruction over the years has suggested that golfers should swing their arms freely through the ball, that the arms should start the down swing.

From my point of view, the arms are moved freely, and there is a big difference between *moving your arms* and *having them moved freely.* (arms *are moved* freely.)

You are asked to look at pictures of a good swing, and it is pointed out that the space between the right shoulder and the hands gets larger as the swing moves forward. Some instruction says that this is proof that the arms start the swing forward. Yes, the space does appear to increase, but you are being misled by what you think you are seeing. From the front angle, or looking from the position facing the golfer's chest and waist, it does appear that the space gets larger, but it is an optical illusion.

When the swing is well on its way in its forward motion, (Picture B on page 69) the right arm is folded at the same angle as it was at the top of the swing. Also, the hands are the same distance from the right shoulder as they were at the top. What has happened is that the hands, arms, and club, as a unit, have been moved forward by a transfer of weight that comes from the body (*inside*) moving forward.

Ben Hogan said, when describing his forward swing at the half way point, "My arms are in the same relative position as they were at the top of the swing. My body did its work on the down swing by pulling the arms and hands into position. Forget about your arms, hands, shoulders and club when starting the down swing."

John Schlee, in his book Maximum Golf, *said he asked Ben Hogan about pronation and supination. Hogan looked at John and said, "Forget about that. Let your shoulders move your arms, everything else is pure reaction. On the back turn, the right palm points at the sky and the left palm at the ground. Keeping the arms inward on the target turn causes the hands and wrists to react and square the club face. Through the hitting area, the right palm works down at the ground."*

Note how the unit (hands, arms and club) stay in place as it is moved forward by transferring weight. This unit does not move on its own.

Do not be misled. It is just the angle you are watching from. Look at the swing from in back or behind, and you can see the hands stay in the same relative position to the right shoulder until the expanding action from centrifugal force takes over. As the swing moves forward toward ball contact, the arms begin to expand or stretch out to an expanded position. Keep in mind that centrifugal force is an expanding motion, and the arms of a golfer expand for the same reason a baseball pitcher's arm expands. The body (*inside*) is doing its job of moving forward, transferring weight that causes the natural results of the laws of physics to take place. Also, (in picture C on page 69) the hands, arms, and club start to move forward very quickly and powerfully, again a natural result of the *inside moving the outside,* not because the golfer is trying to swing his arms fast. Angular Momentum is doing its part at this point in the swing, and this is another reason there is no need to try and do anything with your hands or arms during the swing.

The Outside

On page 21 we explained Angular Momentum; the rotation of matter or mass around its axis or center.

In the golf swing the "axis" of rotation is our spine, or a line midway between the shoulders. The "mass" of the swing is made up of the body, shoulders, arms, hands, and club. At the top of the backswing a large part of the mass (hands, arms, and club) moves very close to the axis of the swing, our spine. The right arm is flexed and is very close, and the left arm could not be closer. Then when the transfer of weight or turn starts the swing going forward, momentum is created by this rotational action.

As the arms and club are being brought forward, they begin to move away from the axis of the body. This is a result of the centrifugal force that is being created by *the inside moving the outside* and thus causing expansion of the arms. As the forward swing continues, the hands and arms keep moving further from the axis and angular momentum (a law of physics) starts to first slow down your arms, then your hands. The momentum the arms and hands once had moves out into the club head and creates power and club head speed automatically without any conscious effort by the golfer. Keep in mind, the tip end of a whip gets all its speed from *the handle.*

is expanding.

Remember, when a golf swing has angular momentum, the hands are actually slowing down when the ball is hit. Some golfers feel the hands are or should be speeding up at this point; they are not - in a sound swing the hands are slowing down because of angular momentum.

Like the tip end of a whip, the club head now has all the momentum, speed, and energy.

A very good swing thought is to feel the arms are very light during the swing.

TARGET TURN: BEFORE TURN . . .

In my opinion, the body will always turn - it is a natural tendency. Some golfers will turn *too soon*, some *too late*. Others do *not turn* enough, but there always is some semblance of a turn in the down swing. Because there is some type of turn going on, a good key to have is to just go forward with your lower spine, and after you start going forward, the natural tendency to turn will become part of the forward swing. In all sound swings, the lower spine moves forward before it starts to turn (see illustration A, B and C). Just let the lower spine go forward and the rest will take care of itself. Keep the inside moving until the right side is closer to the target than the left.

There are many visualizations good golfers use to get the lower body to start the transfer of weight forward.
- Move the left knee to the target.
- Move the left hip with a turn of the left leg.
- Some very fine teachers feel the instinct to go forward is so strong that you do not have to think about it at all.

Our down swing must also stay on its plane or path, have width or extension (in fact expanding extension), and finish on balance with the right side closer to the target than the left. All these prerequisites will occur when the arms do nothing consciously in the front swing.

Down swing should feel the same speed as the back swing. Do not try to make the down swing go faster; don't try and add speed. When you let the lower body or weight transfer (*inside*), bring the hands, arms, and club down, they will have unbelievable power and speed because they are being moved under the laws of motion. The change of direction (when the swing stops going back and starts forward) is slow in a sound swing.

BASE OR FIXED POINT

Your target turn needs a base of support or fixed point to move around. In a sound golf swing the left foot is this base.

This base can be seen in all sports. The left foot anchors or gives the needed support for the movements forward in sports. Try to move forward without first establishing a base of support for turn and weight transfer that should be present. If the left foot is not in place first, this will be very hard to accomplish.

In golf, some outstanding players keep their left foot in place during the back swing. You too may want to try this, but if you find this thought does not fit into your style, please be sure to return your left foot to the ground to support your turn forward.

RIGHT SHOULDER MOVES RIGHT ELBOW DOWN PLANE. THIS MOVES THE LOWER SPINE FORWARD TO BACK OF BALL BEFORE HIP TURN STARTS.

Remember how slow the body of the baseball batter, pitcher or fielder is moving, but how fast the hands and arms are being moved.

BASE OR FIXED POINT

THE HEAD

During the backswing, if your head moves back a little, this is very acceptable to me. It is very hard to make a backswing that transfers weight with the head staying steady. In fact, you may find yourself making what you feel is a very acceptable backswing, but with most of your weight still forward if the head does not move back a little. A very common fault among recreation golfers is trying to keep the head still during the backswing.

On the forward swing, your head must stay back as the body brings the swing forward. The head is the fulcrum of the swing.

Example:

Picture a baseball player's head going forward with the bat as he makes his swing. If the head goes with the arms and bat as his body is turning forward, the swing will have little power. With the head back, acting as the swing's fulcrum, the bat receives the energy of centrifugal force and has lots of power.

Example:

Picture a hammer in use, with the handle and head staying together as you try to hit something. There would be very little power. The handle is the fulcrum, and therefore must stay behind as the head passes it to have any energy created.

The same is true of the golf swing. Its fulcrum (head) must stay back until the ball is on its way and then it comes forward because of the pulling energy of centrifugal force. The head comes forward only after the ball is on its way. In one of Alex Morrison's old books, he made a suggestion that I use for myself and have used in teaching for years. "Keep the chin pointed behind the ball until the ball is on its way."

Right Side is closer to target than left.

LOOKING AT THE SWING
FROM BEHIND CAN HELP

This is an illustration of Bobby Nichols' swing - but anyone's sound swing could have been used.

Note pictures #1 and #9 - They are the same; but #1 is at address, while #9 is at ball contact.

Note picture #3 and #8 - They are the same; but #3 is on the way back, while #8 is in the front swing.

Note picture #4 and #7 - they are the same; but #4 is on the way back, while #7 is in the front swing.

Note in pictures 1 thru 10 - the hand and arms (*outside*) are in the same relative position as the upper body (*inside*).

It can be helpful to picture the hands, arms and club as "a unit," let's say the letter Y or a triangle. You can see the "unit" does not move on its own. The "unit" is moved by the *inside* and stays in place because of inertia.

Yes, the hands fall under the club at the top and the arms expand during the front swing. But this happens and is caused by the laws of motion a sound swing is under the influence of. Golfers do not have to do anything consciously with their hands and arms. They should just trust letting the *inside move the outside.* The unit of hands, arms and club will be moved back and forth during the swing in the same relative position it was in at address by the transfer of weight created by the actions of the *inside.*

We can see the same position in the back and front swings because the position the hands, arms and club take at address stays in place and is just moved back and forth by the *inside.*

1

2

3

4

5

6

7

8

9

10

11

12

STANDING TO THE BALL, BALANCE, COUNTER BALANCE AND LOW CENTER OF GRAVITY

At address, your body should and must be somewhat relaxed. Any tension will negate the movement of weight your swing is trying to transfer back and forth.

We like to have golfers stand wide enough to support the weight shift. In most cases this means wider than you think. It will only be too wide if you are outside your shoulders with the feet. Stand nice and wide, with knees pointed slightly to the target, left foot turned out, and right foot square.

When the set-up is complete, I like the weight to be more to the heels than toes and slightly more to the left side (for a right-handed golfer).

Your legs should have a flex at the knees for balance. At times, golfers bend their knees in a way that makes the lower stomach and thigh go forward to the ball. From this kind of leg stance, your lower body cannot perform as it should.

Your buttocks is out past the heels a few inches as you bend the upper body over the hips with your back staying straight. (feel like you are squatting)

Your hands and arms, as you bend over, will move off the body. Gravity will cause them to hang straight down from the shoulders when you bend. The upper arms will stay on your chest, and keep your head and chin up. Your chin should not move closer to the chest when you bend over at address. If it does, the chin will be in the way of the backswing, thus stopping the coil.

The head is placed a little more to your right side than the left. The feeling of having it behind the ball is a good one. I believe in the right elbow pointing just outside right hip at address. When standing in back of a good golfer looking down the target line, you will see the right elbow placed away from the body.

BALANCE

Balance in a golf swing is most important. To be able to make a full swing that is creating power and stays in balance should be the goal of every golfer. In order to have balance you will need *counter balance* and a low *center of gravity*.

When standing to the ball correctly (in balance) your head, shoulders, upper arms, and upper chest will be tilted forward. The total weight of these body parts is sizeable, with this much body weight forward there must be some body weight placed in a position to counter balance it.

The ball is placed just forward of center with the short and mid-irons. Forward of this position with the longer clubs.

Try not grounding the club-head. With the club on the ground you cannot feel the weight of the club - just hold the clubhead an inch or so off the ground, and this will let you feel the weight of the clubhead that the inside is going to move back and forth.

Standing to ball, back is straight, chin is up, buttocks out, and an angle between the arms and club caused by the hands being placed low - not up.

To create this all important *counter balance* in the set-up, a golfer should bend from the hips not the waist. This will insure that the buttocks will move out past the heels, and create the needed counter balance. When bending from the waist there is a good chance you will not create a proper counter balance in your posture or set-up.

Balance is also a result of a *low center of gravity*. A low center of gravity is as important to successful shot making as *any* element of the swing we could discuss. It has been proven scientifically and reputably, kinesiology professors would agree, balance and a low center of gravity go hand-in-hand.

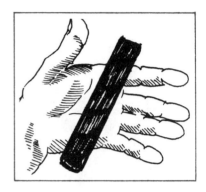

In professional sports, the athletes who have outstanding balance or are difficult to knock off balance, all have low centers of gravity.

Golfers who are able to keep balance throughout the swing, have the proper set-up, low centers of gravity, and then make the swing *without changing* that address position. (They swing without going up or down; they swing without changing the center of gravity). The center of gravity for a golfer is located in the lower back. During the swing, this area should stay level. A quick start or change of direction can contribute to a loss of balance.

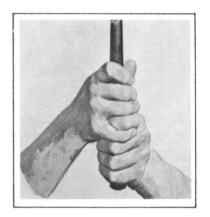

Some golfers make the mistake of putting the right hand on the club by reaching out and over the chest with the right arm and shoulder. This puts another stop sign on your backswing (like a chin that is too low). Your right shoulder will prevent a good coil from this position. (Put the right hand on the club without reaching across the chest.)

The feet, knees, hips, and shoulders are all on the same line pointing in the same direction, just left of the target or open at address.

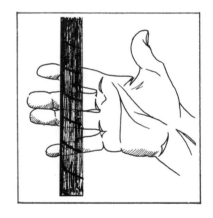

Some very fine teachers like to have the shoulders pointing *more to the left than hips and feet.* You may want to try this. These teachers feel you can make a bigger, natural coil from the shoulders pointing left at the start of the swing.

I like golfers to feel that their arms are very light, not tight or heavy, and they should stay that way during the entire swing. The arms are moved back and forward, and if they are tight or heavy, they cannot move as they should.

HOLDING THE CLUB

Holding the club correctly is most important, but in my view, it is not as complicated as some make it sound.

First, I prefer the words "holding the club," rather than "gripping the club." Gripping sounds like you must apply strength - you do not.

Just hold the club in your left hand so it crosses the lower palm of the hand while your fingers coil around the club. The club will be on the correct angle if it lies just under the heel pad of your hand and across the pad of the carpal bone of the forefinger.

With the right hand, the club is held only in the fingers. We prefer having our students use the OVERLAP rather than the INTERLOCK style when holding the club. It has been my experience that when a golfer joins the pinky of the right hand with the forefinger of the left, he holds on with these two fingers and will sometimes let go with the rest of his fingers during the swing.

Our suggestion is to place the pinky of the right hand over the forefinger of the left. (Just lay it there, NO PRESSURE). There should be nine fingers on the club with this style, with the left thumb just right of center, and the right thumb just left of center. Palms of hands face each other.

V's of grip (lines formed by the thumb and forefinger) point to chin or the right side of the body.

I know a lot has been written about how much pressure should be used when holding the club. I feel there should be no extra pressure. Just hold the club. When extra pressure is applied, you are going to stop the natural movements of your swing, along with the natural movements that occur in the hands as the swing loads up going back, and then expands going forward. Extra pressure in the hands would be like several girls in the middle of a skate line standing very rigid with the rest of the girls on the line being relaxed. You can see how these girls in the middle would take away from the natural movement and power of a skate line.

Back of left hand and club face are in line with each other, pointing to the target, with a small natural inward bend in the left wrist.

THE CLUB BECOMES LONGER, SO ITS FORWARD NOT DOWN

Over the years, many students whom I have worked with tell me they want to learn to hit down on the ball and take divots the way the professional golfers they watch and admire do.

From my point of view, divots are fine, (the best swings produce thin divots) but trying to hit down will destroy the forward swing. Anytime the body is being asked to go in two directions at the same time, something will go wrong. You should only be trying to go forward to the target, not down to the ball during this phase of the swing.

Yes, sound swings do take divots, but its because the club becomes longer during the forward swing then it was at address. With this added length, the swing then takes a divot automatically, without trying to HIT DOWN.

Explanation:

At address the end of the grip is a measurable distance from the ground. This distance is shorter than the clubs actual length for two reasons:

1. At address the club is not placed at a perpendicular angle.
2. The club is designed so that the grip end falls forward of the clubhead and ball at address.

These two conditions and the natural actions of a sound swing are the reasons you should *not* be trying to hit down.

As a sound swing is making ball contact, the club, arms, and wrists are *about* to become *fully extended* and *stretched out*; the right shoulder is *lower* than it was at address; and soon the hands will no longer be in front of the clubhead, all causing the club to become longer than it was at address letting the swing take a divot.

The natural or automatic result of a sound swing is a club that becomes longer than it was at address, (by at least ½ inch) and takes a divot after ball contact. There is no need to try and hit down in a sound swing, expansion creates divots as the club becomes longer. (Keep in mind that centrifugal force is also pulling the clubhead down and out.)

Address

SMALL WHEEL

When the angle is retained, your swing will have what could be called a "small wheel." In a factory that has conveyor belts, the belt that moves around a small wheel travels faster than a belt that moves around a larger wheel.

When the angle in your swing is retained, it is similar to the small wheel conveyor belt. Your hands and club travel around a small wheel before ball contact at top speed.

When the angle of your swing is not retained, it is similar to the big wheel conveyor belt, and your hands and club travel around a large wheel before ball contact at a slower rate.

Fully Extended

BIG WHEEL   SMALL WHEEL

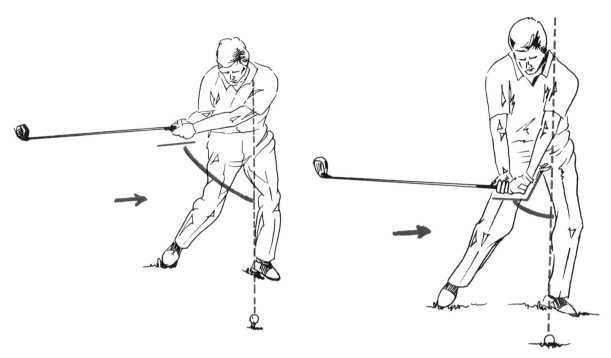

MASS - VELOCITY - ENERGY - LEVERAGE

The energy of an object in motion is called "Kinetic Energy." During a golf swing, Kinetic Energy has an affect on the clubhead.

Energy is defined as "the ability to do work." In golf, this work is the ability to move the ball. This formula in physics is (MV^2) or Mass times Velocity. It then follows, the greater the "Kinetic Energy" of the clubhead the further the ball goes.

Keep in mind that there are only two elements in this formula; Mass (clubhead weight) and Velocity (clubhead speed). That's all! Only mass and speed; no strength, power, or coil for tension.

Once a golfer has the club in his/her hands, the mass cannot be changed, only the velocity of the swing can be influenced during the swing. So, how can, or what is the best way for a golfer to affect the velocity of the clubhead so that it can achieve maximum speed? The answer is Leverage.

Physics tells us we need a mechanical advantage. In a sound swing, this advantage will come from "the Law of the Lever." This law states "force is multiplied by the length of the lever - the longer the lever, the greater the multiplier."

For a golf swing to have its longest lever or largest multiplier that can accelerate the club to its greatest velocity, the "lever force" must be applied from a point as far away from the clubhead as possible.

The furthest distance from the clubhead is the center of the spine between the shoulders. This center must become the pivot point of the swing for maximum multiplication of the Laws of Leverage.

When the swing comes from a rotating center it *will* have the leverage that can create maximum velocity in the front swing. The longer the lever, the greater the speed. (You will not have the longest lever if the hands start the swing; start with your inside, not hands or arms.)

The backswing is also affected by the laws of leverage. During the final stages of this part of the swing, the club slows down because the *wrists have flexed* and the *right arm has folded*, causing the lever of the swing to shorten and this naturally slows down the clubhead.

When a golfer is said to be "hitting" or "casting" from the top, they have produced velocity too early in the front swing. If the wrists are not allowed to flex early in the backswing, the lever of the swing stays extended too long and the backward movement of the clubhead does not slow down to an acceptable change of direction speed, causing a hit or casting from the top.

When a golfer adds length to the lever of the swing early or too soon, there will be little or no velocity when the clubhead reaches the ball. Again, start your front swing with your INSIDE for maximum clubhead speed.

A Sound Backswing Has Extension and Width.

When the inside moves the outside you can see a space between the arms (outside) and the body (inside) at the start of a sound backswing that has width and extension. (Soon the right arm will start to fold and wrists will start to flex.)

In a sound front swing, the right leg leads the hands. The hands and arms are also in the same position in a baseball swing.

TRUST A WEIGHT TRANSFER

Our suggestion in clinics or on the lesson tee to golfers is to just trust transferring weight back and forth. Do not try to hit the ball or be preoccupied with several swing thoughts. Learn the feel of a correct weight transfer and try and copy that feel every time you swing. The longer the shot, the more weight you should move back and forth.

Spend time learning the grip, stance, and correct alignment. This is going to take a fair amount of time, so be prepared.

You do not have to get overly involved in the swing theory. When your *inside is moving your outside*, the laws of physics and math create a sound swing.

A good example of the proper weight transfer happens when a baseball player is in the ON DECK CIRCLE warming up with a few bats. He is just turning his weight back and forth and the arms and bats are going along for the ride.

The arms just seem to flow back and forth as the body moves them. This is what your swing should feel - "light."

If you look closely at this baseball player warming up, watch how the bats are the last to come forward, moved by the transfer of weight as the body turns forward.

You may want to take two clubs and recreate the movements of a baseball player at the on deck circle. Make sure your arms are relaxed and light, and make no attempt to move them. Just turn back and forth and the arms and clubs will be moved by the body turning weight back and forth.

This is pure, *inside moving the outside*, as it happens in the golf swing and other sports. Your swing will have extension, width, coil, stay on its plane, retain its angle and have a balanced finish with the right side closer to the target than the left when the *inside moves the outside*.

REVIEW

Your golf swing, as I said before, is very personal to you. It may have been developed with thoughts and ideas that were more involved than what I have given you here.

To be sure, there is more than one way to learn a skill, any skill.

The ideas and suggestions given here have taken years to develop and recognize. The end product is not a new way to swing a club, nor is it based on any new golf secrets. The information is simple, sound and worthwhile, and it has helped golfers at every level make progress.

The reason, or one reason it feels easy and smooth when you toss a bean bag underhand to a target, (easier than when you throw a dart at a target) is because the motion of the bean bag toss is a transfer of weight and a dart throw is not.

A dart toss comes to a sudden stop, (similar to the unsound golf swing) whereas the bean bag toss, at its finish, feels light and relaxed (similar to the sound golf swing). At the end of the bean bag toss, you cannot quite feel its finish, it's energy into nothingness. This is unlike the dart toss that you can feel come to a sudden stop because it's a hand, wrist, lower arm movement that does not have a transfer of weight.

With this approach, the beginner will not have very much to think about. The more advanced player will have a better understanding of what happens and why in a sound swing, and finally the expert golfers will develop a new trust in their swing.

When you trust not thinking about your hands, arms and what the club is doing, golf will become less complicated. It will give you the opportunity to pay attention to playing the game of golf. Thinking about your swing and the ball will not be necessary.

It has been my experience, when golfers start to hit shots they are happy with and they can recognize improvement, some are not comfortable that they are not thinking about their hands, arms and club. It's too simple! Then when they hit a shot they are not happy with, they feel foolish. Such a simple thought, if it is true, why can't I do it "all the time."

Well, golf is not "all the time" for anyone, or any approach.

Keep in mind that when we cannot do something that seems or is somewhat complicated, we will accept our lack of progress and keep working. But when information is given in a very simple way, and we do not get the hang of it - it's only human nature to dismiss this simple thought or suggestion as incomplete or incorrect. Our ego would never admit that we have not worked hard or long enough with the suggestion. Again, it's only human nature.

This approach, with the *Inside Moving the Outside,* is very simple and it works, and will work better the more you work with it. Power in sports is a transfer of weight, and the *outside* (hands and arms) cannot transfer weight, only the *inside* can.

I would like you to think about the way we throw a bowling ball or a frisbee. During the actions or movements of these acts, the only feeling you are aware of is *motion,* until the very end of the act when the ball or frisbee is leaving your hand. At that time you may be feeling power, or speed, or snap.

The same is true in a sound golf swing. There will be no feeling of speed or power during most of a sound swing, golfers should be aware of motion, and only after the ball is on its way should there be a feeling of power or speed.

PROGRESS

We have all known golfers who play what could be called a steady game, and others who truly do not know what to expect from one round of golf to the next. There are golfers who always seem to be improving their game and some who feel they will never see progress. Also, when we first start to play, some of us learn faster than others.

There are men and women who have been playing golf for years (spending a fair amount of money on lessons, equipment, green fees or dues, golf books, magazines, etc.) and still see little or short-lived progress with their golf.

Are some golfers better athletes than others? Do some have better equipment? Are some stronger? I could go on, but perhaps golfers who see faster and lasting progress are "Better Students."

After years of coaching and teaching golf at every level, I have gotten the impression that some golfers do not know what to expect from the lesson experience.

Few golfers understand how or what is involved in making progress with their golf. These men and women may not know that the progress they would like to make in golf is based largely on how *they* meet the responsibility of being a student.

Yes, there are students who do not know how to take or learn from a lesson; but this should be of no surprise. Remember during our school years, very few of us made the progress we were capable of.

Years ago when the famous golf instructor, Tommy Armour, was asked to name golf's best teacher, he answered, "It takes great learners to make reputations for teachers." Instructors have a responsibility, but so does the student.

Today, all over the country, you will find golf instructors doing a fair amount of research on the golf swing. They are traveling distances and incurring the expense to attend teaching workshops. These men and women are enrolling in classes to improve their communication skills. They are learning new drills and exercises to show students how to improve their swings. Investments are also being made in teaching aids and equipment like video replay.

There is a large segment in the profession who are always trying to upgrade their approach to instruction. They want to help golfers get more enjoyment from their games. Still, progress is slow and unseen for many students who say they would like to see improvement.

I honestly feel some students do not realize they must play a large part before, during, and after a lesson, if they are to see improvement in their golf.

Could some of the many lessons given every year in this country improve? Yes! Should some professionals improve what they do and how they do it? Yes! But this OBSERVATION could, and does, go beyond professional golf into any and all professions (law, medicine, banking, etc.).

To hear time and again that the reason for someone's poor golf is because of the way the game is being taught is, in most cases, just an "unfair and misleading" observation.

Perhaps, if I may give some suggestions on how to approach the lesson experience, (before, during, and after) you will receive more from instruction, either from a book, magazine, or a lesson from a professional. When you improve as a student, you will improve as a golfer.

BEFORE

First, prior to taking a lesson, it will help to understand that golf is an acquirable skill. Golf is no different than learning how to type, draw, or play a musical instrument. Like all acquirable skills, golf is LEARNED in steps and stages. But, for some reason, when it comes to learning or improving our golf, the time it is going to take is overlooked. There is a passage from a book, *First Steps to Golf* written in 1913 by G.S. Brown, that I would like to share with you. "The old proverb that it is necessary for a child to walk before it runs is absolutely true on the links. At the present time, one sees thousands of Golf Children trying to run, when in reality they cannot walk."

Before going to your appointment for instruction, realize it is just that; a session of instruction. It is not a test. Some golfers try very hard to make a good impression on their coach. Please do not be concerned about how you are going to look to your coach. You are not going to embarrass yourself. Relax and be yourself and the lesson will go just fine. Remember . . . it is not a test.

Before getting started with lessons it helps to know any progress a student is going to make is because of work. It is the teamwork between you and your coach that produces the results that both are looking for. Students must also work on their own. A coach can impart knowledge, but skill must come from the student.

Golf is a game of control based on self control. As you start to learn and gain experience, remember, this alone will not lead to progress. It is what you do with this knowledge and experience you have gained that leads to the progress you are looking for in your game.

Studies tell us it takes seventeen (17) days for a factory worker to learn a new habit, and forty-five (45) days to replace an old habit with a new one.

There are very few golfers who have seventeen days in a row, much less forty-five days to spend working on a change the instructor has suggested. So, be prepared and understand that the learning process takes time. Your style or approach to your swing can change and improve, but it will take some time and work. Also, keep in mind, it takes longer to unlearn an old habit and then learn a new one.

Early in 1980, the great Jack Nicklaus made a commitment to make a change in what he called "a long standing golfing fault" in his swing. Jack, in describing the work, time and effort, said, "It was not a joyful experience."

Next, before you make an appointment for your lesson, try and gather some information about the coach. Some professionals give a large volume of lessons and this can be an indication of their skill. Find out if this coach is teaching a wide range of golfers: men, women, and high and low handicappers. The golf swing is the same for all, but the approach to coaching should vary with each student. Also, find out what kind of teaching aids may be available (T.V., replay, etc.).

A good source for obtaining the name of a "Qualified Instructor" is other golfers. You may see or play with someone who's game you like; ask where they have taken lessons. If you feel the golf staff at the club or course where you play most of your golf, and who see you on a regular basis, are not the ones who can help with your game, ask them to make a suggestion on who you could make an appointment with. Take the time to find a coach you feel can do the job; someone who is going to take a real interest in you and your golf game.

The final "Before" suggestion . . . there is a very good chance you will feel you are not improving, or perhaps even regressing after taking lessons. This is only natural. But if you are aware of this feeling before taking your lessons, you have started to understand the whole lesson experience.

DURING

Be on time for your lessons. At times, the lesson before yours will run a little long; you could use the time while you wait to start your lesson to warm up. But if you are late, everyone's appointment for the day will be off schedule.

When first meeting with your coach, I suggest you tell him/her what you would like to work on during your time together. At times, you will suggest one area, only to have the coach suggest working in a different area first.

Do not take over the lesson — let the coaches do their job. At times, a coach when trying to be polite to a member of his club, is intimidated and backs off. As the student, do not let this happen and your lesson will be a better one.

You may want to work on the backswing, but your coach wants to talk about something else. Let the coach do the coaching and teaching. Remember, golf is learned in steps and stages. Ask the coach to explain the why and the what of his suggestions.

There are times when we have decided to take a lesson and expect the coach will want us to make a big change in our style. Our game is way off, and we feel it is going to take a big change to bring our game around to familiar standards. Often this is not the case.

Keep in mind the swing you make for the most part is based on your *Grip, Stance, Posture, Alignment,* and *Balance.* So, even though your game is way off its normal level, it may only be a small suggestion about fundamentals that will bring your game back.

In the case of a new golfer, often the required movements of a golf swing that would be considered sound are understood by the student long before a sound grip, proper stance and balance, and correct alignment are learned.

So, both the new and experienced golfer should be prepared to spend a fair amount of time learning these fundamentals.

I know these areas are not as interesting to the golfer as the swing itself, and because of this, they may become less important than they should be. In truth, it is these areas you and your coach should be working on most of the time. These seemingly less important parts, however, *are* the most important. (Grip, Stance, Posture, Alignment, Balance)

You will seldom see a golfer with a bad grip, stance, and balance meet with success.

When a coach asks his students, "What would you like to work on today?", the most common answer is, "I can hit my irons but my woods give me trouble."

Please understand, the swing is the same for both woods and irons. After looking at a few swings with both, my coaching eye will see the same mistake. The only difference is with the shorter iron clubs; the mistake is smaller than with the larger wood clubs. Students are misled by the shot that is only 6 yards left or right and still hit the green with an iron, not realizing that the same swing with the wood would produce a shot that is 15 or 20 yards off line. So, "Let's work on the woods" is the student's suggestion.

Do not be unhappy when your coach wants to work on the fundamentals of golf, (stance, alignment and balance) because he and you are headed in the right direction.

When making swings during your lesson, it may be helpful for you to understand that because you cannot see yourself swing, you are making a swing that is different than the one you think you are making. We can also be misled by what we are feeling when making a swing.

It is important that you and your coach work together until you understand and can mentally see the same swing. (T.V., replay or Poloroid pictures can be very helpful in this area.)

If you have a Polaroid camera or T.V. recorder, bring it with you to your lesson (if your coach does not have these available). Take a picture at address, at the top of your backswing, and at your finish. I am sure these pictures will help you understand the suggestion your coach is making.

If you see some progress during your lesson, this is fine. But do not be disappointed if you do not. The suggestions given in a lesson may take some time for your own style and feel to adjust to.

When working with a new suggestion, never, and I mean never, say to yourself, "This feels funny or awkward." This would be a negative thought. Just say, "Well this feels new and I will give myself some time," or "When I have more experience I will do better."

Percy Boomer told us, "Habit, good or bad, in golf or outside of it, needs time to consolidate."

During a lesson, ask questions and take notes. Get your coach to give you several different word pictures of what he would like you to do. When you have more than one way or thought to make something happen in the swing, you will add an element to your game that can only help. Your body cannot teach you a thing, only the mind can.

When taking a lesson you may hit some very nice shots, but you may feel this will not happen on the course. This is sometimes true, but after more practice and coaching you will be able to bring your practice range swing to the golf course.

During the lesson, your coach will probably want to make one or two suggestions. Do not feel short changed. We can only practice one part of the swing at a time; more than that and the lesson would be less helpful.

At the completion of your lesson, ask what questions you would like, and then find out when your instructor would like to see you again.

When working on your golf game, please do not forget the short game. Pitching, chipping and putting make up over 60% of the swings we make in a round of golf. Coaching in this area may be more helpful in lowering your score than the long game coaching.

AFTER

What students do after a lesson will make a difference in the type of progress they will see.

It is important to have a clear understanding of the suggestions your coach made about your style. But it is what you do with those suggestions that is going to make a difference in your game.

I would not suggest going out to play a round of golf immediately after a lesson. Suggestions made in a lesson must be worked on for a while on a practice range. By the way, I think there should always be more practice than playing when it comes to golf. I will explain.

Let's look at the round of golf that the score of 100 is made. You are on the course for 4 to 4½ hours, and take 2 putts per hole. That leaves 64 shots, of which let's say, 14 are chip or short shots, around the green. This would leave 50 full swings. Fifty full swings are one pail of balls at a practice range, that takes twenty minutes to one-half hour to hit. In fact, because each ball takes only a few seconds to put in place and hit, you could say 50 full swings is only 5 or 6 minutes actually of swing time.

You have been on the course for hours, but only minutes of swing time to show for it. Can you imagine only practicing typing for minutes each week? Progress would be very slow. So our suggestions to any golfer, whether you are working on a new suggestion or trying to keep your game in shape, is to always have more swing time off the course than on. A few hours of practice time is like playing several rounds of golf.

When playing golf, tips from others are as free as the rain from the sky. Please do not be a willing target for them. Friends mean well, but they are going to slow the learning process down. You will only drown in these well meaning suggestions.

At the practice range or on the course, your main challenge will be to keep using the suggestions your coach has given even when you are hitting poor shots.

Poor shots are part of the learning process. It's like misspelling a word. Remember that it is how we learned how to spell — by misspelling.

There is a point where golf is really a "self-taught game." We need a coach to show us what we should be working on — but when we start to practice and pay attention and remember, we are teaching ourselves the game. In a sense, good coaches cannot teach you, but they can show you how to learn. I feel this is the cornerstone of the "After" lesson segment of the lesson experience. We teach ourselves when we practice correctly. Keep in mind you will have your ups and downs, your good and bad days. Any and all golfers, at every level, experience ups and downs throughout their personal golfing history. Understand your golf game will always be hot and cold. Your challenge is to bring the two natural extremes together more often than not. Also, learn some days are better than others.

When on the course playing, do just that — play golf. Do not get overly involved with swing theory. Pay attention to your alignment, your grip, and then swing. Save theory for the practice range; on the course play golf. Ask your coach for tips on taking your game and style to the course.

When on a practice range take your time between swings. Do not hit ball after ball quickly. Take your time. Think about the suggestion you and your coach are working on. Always hit to a target, this is a *must* if your practice is to be useful.

We feel most golfers fail to reach their potential not because of a lack of talent as golfers, but it is the inability to be a good student that can hold golfers back. I hope the suggestions made here will help with your understanding of the lesson experienced.

I truly feel most golfers can reach their potential when they improve as students of the game.

Part II

OBSERVATIONS FOR YOUR PROGRESS

Understanding your goals beforehand will help with any endeavor you may choose. Golf is no exception. D.A. Forgan, a Scottish professional, said of golf, "It's a science — the study of a lifetime in which you may exhaust yourself but never the subject." Ben Hogan said, "Every year we learn a little more about golf. Each chunk of knowledge paves the way to greater knowledge."

In the academic world they are called prerequisites, classes that must be taken before you can go on to the next subject. I feel golf has some prerequisites. Greater enjoyment and progress will come to the golfers who not only make a study of golf techniques, but also some understanding of golf's prerequisites.

There is more to playing golf than hitting the ball. Before progress can come, you should be aware of these prerequisites; in fact, the earlier in your golfing career the better.

For a new golfer, your efforts to improve will be more productive. If you have been playing for some time, it will help you to understand your past golfing experiences when you are aware of golf's prerequisites.

Progress and enjoyment from golf will be aided when we realize that being discouraged and golfing go hand in hand. To be discouraged is to be someone who plays golf. "How long will it take to learn?" "How many lessons will it take?" "How can I play the front nine so well and the back nine so poorly?" "Why good one day, bad the next?" These are the questions discouraged golfers are always asking.

FACT. The only thing constant about golf is it's inconsistency. A fact for Jack Nicklaus. A fact for me. A fact for you. No one plays well all the time, or even up to their potential. In a round of golf, your game can come and go, just that quickly, to any golfer, professional or amateur. It's the nature of the game.

If you have prepared yourself for the natural ups and downs of golf, you will have made a big step in understanding golf. Golf is not a column of figures that can be added up correctly every time. When you fully recognize that both the new and experienced golfers will have bad days, or bad weeks, or bad months, it will then be easier to break out of your slump.

Progress in golf will always be directly related to the amount of time spent on your game. If your schedule does not permit a whole lot of time for golf, your progress will tend to be slower than someone who has more time.

Even when you are spending what you feel is a lot of time and hard work on your golf game, the progress may be slower than you think it should be. Let us try and help you understand what spending lots of time on your game means.

Ask a golfer how long they have been playing, and you get an answer that will tell you the numbers of years, five, ten, fifteen, followed by "and I still do not break," whatever the golfer's goal is for a score. Let's examine the five year golfer. Suppose he plays an average of twice a week for ten months of the year. That will be eighty times a year or four hundred times over five years. The average score has been 115, with thirty-six putts a round. That would give us a total number of 31,600 golf swings (less putts) over a five year span.

31,600 golf swings is not five years of golf. For one year, it would be 100 swings a day with forty-nine days off. That is less than a tournament professional and some amateurs play in a year and about two years of golf for some serious golfers.

We must realize that most of us are part-time golfers. When you try to improve your game in terms of quality, it's a must that you keep that in mind. It will help you with how you see your progress without being discouraged. If one of your goals is to improve, practice may become more important to you. For sure, PROGRESS will yield to PRACTICE. Golfers who play well, have worked very hard.

YOUR NERVOUS SYSTEM AND GOLF

Playing golf under pressure or when you are nervous, is something all good golfers have learned to do. To make progress in this area, we must first learn a little about our nervous system, and then be aware that successful golf is more than paying attention at the first tee.

Your nervous system will have *a greater effect* on your golf than a good set of clubs, top grade balls, or a lesson from a fine instructor. The effect will either be positive or negative. Before every swing, while preparing to play your next shot, the nervous system will play a major part in the results.

A quote from *Dynamic Anatomy and Physiology*, a book used by medical students, makes this point clearly.

"The nervous system is remarkably wide spread throughout the body. NERVE IMPULSES may be transmitted along the network, virtually from one end to the other. Thus, the activities of one body region are QUITE LIKELY to influence the events in another, and therefore the whole must be considered in any careful examination of activity within a part."

Controlling or having a consistent golf game is controlling or having a consistent nervous system. Small or distant distractions can be as damaging as closer and larger ones. It may take some work on your part, but the results, for sure, will be worth the effort. You can be in the "State of Grace" ready to make smooth swings, with rhythm and grace.

SLOW DOWN, TAKE YOUR TIME, PACE YOURSELF, not only as you step up to the first tee, but the SLOW DOWN must start long before you even get to the golf course. Golfers who rush to the course will not play up to the level they would have had they taken their time. THAT IS A FACT, A MEDICAL FACT, not just a guess.

For some, preparation for a round of golf should start the night before. Other golfers may find when they first get up in the morning is time enough. You see, the medical profession knows that what we do in ONE part of our body of life, will have an effect on other parts. Successful golfers must educate themselves on the working of their nervous systems.

At times, events away from the course can affect our play. I have seen golfers who have gone through a change in their lives, (death of a family member, divorce, money problems, etc.) and either after or during these times, their golf does not reach the level they were once familiar with.

Most golfers go to the course to enjoy and have a good time. So go and enjoy. But approach this day of golf in the same manner you approach other days in your life when the purpose is to enjoy yourself (like going to the beach or out for a visit with friends).

The first thought that may come to mind, (when off to the beach), or is suggested by someone else, is "O.K., let's go - we can relax and have a good time. It will give you time to relax." The key word is relax.

If you start off by leaving on time for the course, you will not have to run from your car to the first tee. You will have time for a warm-up. Hit some practice balls. Practice a little putting. Before you start the round, a warm-up is a must. You will not play to your capability unless you warm-up and get your FEEL and TOUCH going beforehand. If a practice area is not available, do a few exercises to warm-up your body.

On the course, remember to keep in touch with the pace of your game. Try not to make any real quick movements. Do not yell or get excited. Do not grab clubs from your bag. Take them out slowly. Do not run to the next tee. Walk. Try not to get very excited about a good shot, or very mad at the bad ones. Be in control of your nervous system. Remember, what you're doing with one part of your body will have an effect on other parts. Golf is a game played in the "State of Grace," not only from the start of your round, but several hours before.

You cannot let your nervous system get overly involved with what you are trying to do in golf. Pick the club that you feel can get the job done. Then address the ball in a relaxed manner and swing. Do not start thinking about any trouble your shot could get you into. Likewise, you cannot let your body get all keyed up trying to make a "Birdie." Stay calm and keep it simple and you will hit more good shots than ever before.

After the shot has been played, the same approach must be used. Do not get worked up over bad shots. Find the ball and try to do your best with the next swing. Remember the feel of your good swings and repeat the feel. A good shot can also get a golfer emotionally worked up. Try not to let this happen. Keep your mind on what you are doing.

When you have more control over your nervous system, your golf game will have more control. Keep yourself in the "State of Grace." Smooth and easy does it. Take notes the next time you see a professional tournament. Recognize that there is very little emotion to be seen.

THINKING - IT MAY BE THE SECRET

Physical actions occur after a mental message has been sent from our brain to our body. A golfer often will credit a good round to his mental approach or the way he was thinking. A champion golfer once said, "I have found that success on the course depends on the way you think." Another champion said, "The mind always has to operate before the muscles go to work, and the muscles must only operate once the mind is working."

A dictionary defines *thinking* in the following way: "To form or conceive in the mind; To have in mind an idea, image, conception; To analyze or examine; To bear in mind; To recollect or remember; To form a plan."

Listed is only part of the long definition that appears in most dictionaries. But, have we discovered the "Secret" of good golf when we refer to Thinking? Well, maybe. "Thinking" belongs high on the list of essentials for good golf. For sure, you cannot learn or play golf without the thinking process.

For our purpose, let's talk about four parts of the thinking process that come into play most frequently for a good golfer. CONCENTRATION, RECOLLECTION, IMAGINATION, and ANTICIPATION. These are Right side hemisphere functions.

CONCENTRATION: It's standard equipment with all golfers, a must when you are trying to improve or just starting to learn. You MUST pay attention to what you are doing when playing, practicing, taking a lesson, or reading a book on golf. Try to make golf the only thing you are thinking about. Golf will always be more of a mental challenge than a test of your physical skill.

Concentration starts with thinking positively, both on the course and when practicing. On the course think about one shot at a time. Do not replay past shots that were poor. Fear of trouble will break your concentration. Take your time. Do not rush into your swing. Picture what you are trying to do. Wind, distance uphill, downhill, etc., should be taken into consideration before every shot.

When practicing, again take your time between swings. When you are taking the correct approach to your practice session, a small bucket of balls will take over a half-hour and sometimes longer. CONCENTRATE and PICTURE only one part of your swing. Trying to think about several parts at the same time will slow down the progress that your practice session should give you.

RECOLLECTION: Some golfers can tell you shot for shot, a round of golf they played several years ago. If you tend to forget things about your golf that will be helpful in the future, it's time to change. Remembering things about the course you are playing: fast greens, traps you cannot see, uphill and downhill lies, etc., will be very helpful.

If you cannot recall the speed of greens, (so you can keep your touch or feel from hole to hole); if you cannot remember how far you can hit a particular club; if you cannot remember distances; if you cannot recall what your shot will do in the wind; if you cannot recall the feel of your good swings, you are making golf harder than it should be, and it will be very hard for you to improve.

One of the most important uses of recollection comes when trying to repeat a shot you hit a few holes ago or last week. If you cannot remember your grip, posture, or what the swing felt like, your chances of hitting a shot that will come off the way you want are very low. So let's start taking mental notes or even writing things down. All tournament golfers have a set of notes. Notes on the golf course, such as its greens and its distances, are always helpful. But you will find good players also make notes about their golf swing. Recollection is a most important part of good golf.

IMAGINATION: Defined by the dictionary as "The action of forming mental images or concepts of what is not actually present. The creation of new images directed at a specific good or aiding in the solution of problems." Imagination is a mental tool that is always helpful, especially when we have hit the ball into trouble. Every golfer will find trouble from time to time, but some seem to handle it better than others.

At times you have to make up a shot or a swing. The ball is in a spot that no orthodox approach would be useful. First, you should probably be just trying to put the ball back to a place where your normal swing can be used. To do this is sometimes going to take a little imagination.

You may have to turn the club face over, or you may have to stand on one foot, or you may have to hold the club one handed. You may have to swing backwards. Any one of a number of approaches can be helpful at times.

When practicing, sometimes I will make up shots, and try different stances, so they will not be entirely new when I try them on the course. Most common trouble shots include a ball that finds its way under a tree in a spot that gives you little chance to make a full swing. Get down on your knees and swing the club around yourself like a baseball bat. You now will be able to make ball contact and get the ball out of trouble.

Always be thinking and let your natural imagination help with some of those shots that look impossible.

ANTICIPATION: The mental choices you make before your swing will effect the outcome of the shot more than the swing. You must be on guard not to anticipate hitting a shot you have not been successful with before. Play within yourself. Do not try to win with one swing. The golfer who can anticipate the bounce or roll of a shot beforehand, is increasing his chances of a good result. But the golfer who anticipates a result that would be far beyond his normal capabilities, is only asking for more trouble. To try to anticipate the results is very helpful, but don't be unrealistic. Playing within your capabilities is the key to good golf. The winner makes the fewest mistakes.

WATCH - LEARN - AND COPY

An effective way to improve your golf can be by watching good golfers and copying what they do. Most of what we learned as children came from copying others. So why not golf? My suggestion is to watch good golfers. Go to professional tournaments, when you can, and see how they play.

When you see all these good players, the first observation will be that they all look different. Different swings, different sizes. So how can you learn anything? Believe me, if you know what to look for there is lots to be gained from copying good players.

Yes, for sure, they all look different when you do not know what to look for. But when you are looking at some of the fundamentals that exist in all good golfers, they start to look more alike.

A list of observations you should make when watching good players include: Posture, Grip, Head Placement, Leg Work. A Completed Backswing, The Move Forward, and A Routine Before Swing.

POSTURE: Observe and copy how a good player's posture does not change very much from club to club. The only real change is that as the club gets longer, the player is standing farther away from the ball and the feet get wider. But the ball is more or less in the same spot. The arms are the same from the elbow up as they lay on the chest, and the shoulders are the same, with the right lower than the left. The back is in the same straight position. Good players have a small bend from the hips, with their buttocks out just a little with a slight bend at the knees. Please: note the overall lack of tension!

GRIP: Observe and copy how good players do not look like they are holding on for dear life. Their swings have rhythm. If they were holding the club too tightly, they would not have any rhythm. Try holding a pen tightly and see if you can write smoothly. You cannot. So look at the ease with which a good player holds the club. They are very smooth when they do anything with the club.

HEAD PLACEMENT: Observe and copy where a good player places his head. Draw an imaginary line from the left ear down to the ground. You will find that all good players at the start of their swing have their head placed back off the ball (with the tee shot especially). They will keep it back throughout the swing until the ball is hit.

LEGS: Observe and copy the leg action of good players. Your legs are the strongest part of your body. Good players take advantage of the power that is stored in the legs. Most poor golfers have no leg or foot work in their style. So watch how a good golfer's legs are a part of the backswing and are a big help with the forward swing. Every good golfer has his legs working during the entire swing. They are shifting weight back and forth!

BACKSWING: Observe and copy how good players make a weight transfer. Poor goolfers hardly ever transfer weight in the backswing. Look at the turn of good players, club, hands, arms, and shoulders move as a unit. This is a must if your swing is to have the smoothness and power needed to play consistent golf.

CHANGE OF DIRECTION: Observe and copy that when a good player's swing starts forward, it does not pick up a great deal of speed. The start of the forward swing is smooth, just as smooth as the start of the backswing. Good players are not trying to add anything extra to the start of the forward swing. When a poor golfer starts forward, most times it's quick movement without rhythm and grace.

ROUTINE BEFORE SWING: Observe and copy how all good players go through the same pattern of movement before every swing. Consistent golf starts with a constant routine before every shot. Good players feel this repeated pattern of movements will add a repeated pattern to their shots. Every player has a little different routine, but before every shot, the same pattern of movements is repeated.

The next time you see a good player, look for the fundamentals that they all have in common and copy them. All good golfers have different styles. But all good golfers have fundamentals that are very much alike. Your game will improve when your fundamentals improve.

STATE OF GRACE

Golf is a game played in the "State of Grace." I forgot who said it, but that is what most good players feel. They feel graceful. At least most of them do. There is sometimes an exception, but most golfers feel at ease. They feel smoothness. They all worked on trying to achieve this "State of Grace," some more than others. Good players all walk at a pace that helps them stay at ease. Some good players have gone as far as to change their way of life; their way of talking, and where they live. Some have become more involved with religion. All this has been done to gain inner peace which sometimes manifests itself in a golf swing that is in the "State of Grace."

CONTROL

Golf is a game of control. We must try to make our very best shot and our very worst shot very close in quality. The better players hit bad shots, but there is not that much difference between the results of the bad shots and good shots. Thus, the professionals have control built on a few fundamentals.

The game of golf, when played well, is not made up of just GREAT shots, but a game void of bad shots. We will make errors, but we will try not to repeat them. Keep in mind, a golf course is made up of 150 acres, with eighteen different holes, played with fourteen clubs, but with only two types of shots, the long shot and the short shot. It is most important that you keep in mind, at all times, that golf is a target game. Short game thinking, while playing the long game, is sometimes very helpful. No one ever walks onto the green without looking at, or for, the hole or the best line to the hole. So, when walking down the fairway or on the tee, have a target in mind.

IT'S DIFFERENT

There is a big difference between golf and other sports we play. Tennis, baseball, basketball, football, etc., are reaction sports, sports in which the players's movements are controlled and caused by the opponent. In tennis, for example, if the ball goes that-a-way, so must you. And so it is in other sports. But in golf, which is started from a standing still position, the movement is self-imposed. You do not have anyone causing you to move one way or the other. You are on your own. You are not reacting to a ball or man. You have to create a movement. This makes golf a creative performance, not a game where you react.

It's very much like being an actor or actress who walks out on the stage, then begins to perform. The actor's movements are self-created, not a reaction to someone else's movement.

Because the movements of the golf swing are created, any and all elements of being a performer hold true. In my approach to golf instruction, lots of time is spent in this area. Trying to help a golfer improve is much like trying to help an actor become a better performer.

In other sports, where movements are controlled by those whom we are playing with, we are always reacting to the movement of others. In golf we have to think about each shot we will be playing.

If you shot 95, it was not one game but 95 different performances, 95 different times your mind had to tell the body what to do. The golfer, before each shot, must call a play so the body will know what to do.

When the new golfer can recognize the sport of golf as a "Performance," less threatening approaches can be used. On the first tee, with everyone looking on, remember not to think about where the ball will go, but look at the ball and start to FEEL the swing.

Also, the most experienced performers are prepared for a bad performance. They know you can never do something the same way every time. Sometimes the new golfer slows his progress down by trying to hit every shot perfectly. You have to take the bad with the good.

SPLIT EYES AND MIND

Look at the ball, but FEEL or visualize something else. Lots of golfers find themselves looking at the ball and also thinking about it. You cannot play golf and think about the ball.

When you drive a car, you look at the road with your eyes, but we can, at the same time, think about or feel almost anything. Sometimes when on the phone, we can be talking but at the same time thinking about something else. We should use this ability to split our eyes and mind when we play golf.

Look at the ball, but think or visualize what you are going to do or feel in your swing. You have to learn to look at the ball and feel something else.

IT'S IN THE MIDDLE

Recognize that the golf swing has nothing to do with the ball. A golf ball is at the halfway point of the swing, not at the end of the swing. The ball is in the middle. When good players make a practice swing, they are trying to feel the swing and they are trying to repeat the feel of the last shot they were happy with. Also, the practice swing of a good player looks very much like their swing when playing. They are trying to repeat the same swing all the time.

NO ROLL OVER

From my point of view, the progress you are capable of in golf will not take place until there are visualizations of the golf swing in your mind's eye that are helpful. Visualizations that will not mislead!

The subject of wrist "Flex" or "Fold" that takes place as the swing moves *backwards* has already been discussed. This action and why it happens is, for the most part, universally accepted by the teaching and coaching community. This "Flex" or "Fold" during the backswing is one part of the golf swing that has caused little or no controversy over the years.

But as the swing moves forward, movements or positions the hands, arms and wrists go through (unlike the backswing) have been the cause of discussion and debate for years.

"The Right Hand Rolls Over the Left" is a description that has been used for a long time. At times a term is held on to out of convenience, or a "term" has been in use for such a long time, it is felt by some that more harm than good would come out of a change.

In the case of "Rolling the Hands" in the front swing, some of the above are possible reasons that these descriptions are still widely used and believed. But perhaps the strongest case for using these descriptions, these actions (it is said) can be seen when looking at pictures of the swing. Golfers will also say they can feel roll happen.

With all the respect I have for golfers who are working hard to improve, and for all the men and women who teach and coach this game we all love, I would ask them all to take a closer look at pictures of the swing, and maybe statements about rolling the hands would change.

When instruction suggests golfers should be rolling hands, I feel golf is being made harder than it has to be. Yes, there is movement in the hands during the swing, *but it is not a roll over!* Also, the movements that do occur are happening automatically in a sound swing. Golfers are not required to make or put any conscious effort into making these natural movements occur. (There is a natural in plane rotation of the arms in a sound swing.)

As you read on, let's point out again that golfers can very easily be misled by what we think we see, and think we feel. Very easily! When golfers say they can see or feel roll, they are being tricked or misled by their eyes and feel. Also, if feel has not been tied correctly to a picture or visualization, it will always be misleading.

Before explaining what does happen during the front swing to the hands and wrists, it would help if you understand the wrists are very flexible (sometimes called oily) in a sound swing. Because of this flexibility, it is the weight of the club head and centrifugal force that causes hands and wrists to bend or flex into different positions as the swing is in motion. (It is not anything we are doing consciously.)

The first step in understanding what happens to the hands and wrists during the swing is to look at the position they take during the address. Note how the Right Hand has been placed on Top or Over the Left Hand. Also note the lower part of the right arm is above the left arm and there is no forward, backward, up or down bend in the wrists. Let's call this position, center, or on plane.

Your hands are going to stay in this address position throughout the swing (right and on top with no bends) until the weight of the club head causes this relationship to be altered under the laws of motion.

ADDRESS POSITION

The first change we can see (and everyone agrees this change happens) is when the wrists fold as the backswing is reaching its finish.

At the top of the swing the wrist and club can fall into one of three positions - Square, Open, or Closed. Two of these positions open or closed are caused by the club head moving off center or plane.

The club head is square when club head weight is on center or on plane and club shaft is pointing forward or straight with little or *no in* or *out* bend in wrist.

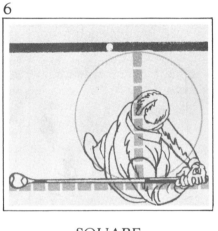

SQUARE

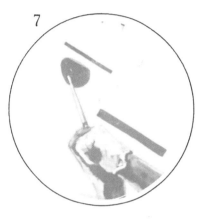

SQUARE

The open position exists when club head weight is right of center. Club shaft points right and wrist bends right.

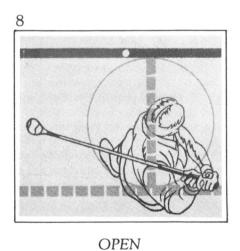

OPEN

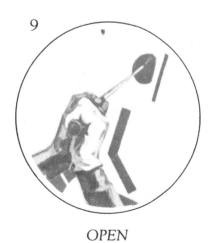

OPEN

The closed position exists when the clubhead weight is left of center. Club shaft points left and wrist bends left.

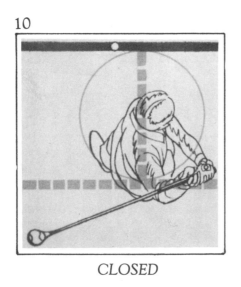

CLOSED

CLOSED

The club head can move off center or plane for several reasons (which we will not go into at this time). But our point and what would be helpful for you to recognize is **the wrists are flexible** and respond to the Laws of Physics and Motion. They will bend in the direction of the club weight and to where the shaft is pointing because of their flexibility.

The positions we can see the wrist fall into during the backswing also occur during the forward motion of a sound swing, and for the same reasons. Wrists do not roll but they will bend left or right of center when the laws of motion cause the flexible wrists to follow the lead of club head weight and shaft. It's Left or Right of center, not roll that takes place when swing is in motion.

Now, let's look at a sound swing as it moves forward and you can see the right hand is still on top because the club is still on center or plane.

As the swing moves to knee or thigh height, the right hand can still be seen on top of the left.

12

13

At impact, the right hand is still on top because the club is still on center or plane.

14

15

16

Sam Snead told John Schlee he played his best golf when his wrists felt "Dead," that the cocked wrists are along for the ride.

As the swing gets waist high this is where the right hand *may look* like it's starting to roll over the left. This is the position that is used most often to show the right is going over the left. The right, any one can see, is higher than the left, *but do not be misled.*

Remember the position the right hand and arm were in at the start of the swing (higher than left). It's still in the same position, (higher); they have not changed. But when looking at pictures of the swing we can be misled into thinking or seeing something that really did not happen, "Roll." (See Picture 1 and 18.)

Also, the club is rising at this point in the swing, which could give the impression the right hand is moving up and over.

17

18

19

20

21

During the next stages of the front swing the centrifugal force and angular momentum that has been created by the rotational movement of the swing starts to influence the club head for the same reasons it did during the backswing, and the club head will start moving left of center. The slinging action of the swing, Centrifugal Force and Angular Momentum are causing this movement to the left by the club head, bending the flexible wrist in the same direction. The wrists are not rolling. Again, it may look like they are from some angles, and maybe feel like they are, but they are following the Laws of Motion and are bending left of center.

A closer look at the position the club, hands and wrists are falling into will show the right hand relationship to the left (on top) has not been altered. We can also see the left wrist is bending in the direction of club head weight. Left of center (not a roll).

22

23

24

25

26

The laws of motion that cause the golf club to move left of center during the front swing are the same laws that cause the "tip end" of a whip to move past the rest of the whip for a short time before the ship becomes fully extended. In an ice show, this same result can also be seen when the outside girl on a skate line is moved past the rest of the line (as she is whipped forward) for a short time just before the line becomes straight. The clubhead is like the tip end of a whip, and is responding to the laws of motion when it moves off center during the front swing. (It goes left of center.)

33

34

35

36

As the swing keeps rotating, about half-way through the follow through, the club head will move back on center, and we no longer will see any bend in the wrists.

The reason this happens is because the club head, during this stage of the swing, is slowing down and the rotating body has again caught up with the club head causing the wrist to come back on center again.

37

38

As the swing moves into its final stages, if a golfer has a full finish the club head responding to the rotation action of a full finish would cause the wrists to bend once again.

39

40

If the hands did roll in the front swing, (right over left) how would the hands finish in their familiar position at the completion of the swing, right under left? There would have had to be some kind of a reroll during the swing, and no swing I have ever seen has had a reroll.

41

42

In closing, for you to be able to make progress with your golf game, you must first see the swing correctly in your mind's eye. If you have been seeing a roll, you may be making golf harder than it has to be.

Yes, there are times when a golfer will try and roll his/her hands or arms to give the ball a big hook. But when your swing is responding to the laws of motion, (with *the inside moving the outside*) the hands, wrists and club without any conscious effort, will fall into all the expected and accepted positions.

When the laws of motion are influencing the swing, your shots will be straight or may have a slight draw without trying to roll. For a short time, the arms of a golfer with a sound swing move closer together during the front swing. This is caused by (A) the outward pull of the club head, (B) expansion, angular momentum and centrifugal force.

You can see the arms move together in pictures of a sound swing (a result of the Laws of Motion). But, during the finish of a swing, the arms will move away or separate from each other once again because the outward pull of the club head, angular momentum, and centrifugal force are *no* longer influencing the swing as the golfer comes to a spent and relaxed finish.

43

Together

44

Separate

Part III

FEEL

I said we were going to talk about feel. What you personally feel as you play is what I am referring to.

Some books have been very good at showing you the "How To" of golf, but they may not be communicating what it "feels" like to play good golf. The written word is digested mentally, and any pictures in a book are digested visually. But we play golf physically.

Good players play by feel or touch. Low handicap and professional golfers can remember the feel of a good golf swing, and have taught themselves to repeat that feel or touch the next time they swing. You have heard it referred to as Muscle Memory; "MUSCLE MEMORY" is "FEEL." It is not memorizing "How To."

"Too much thought about golf mechanics is a bad thing for anyone's game. Now the reason golf is so difficult is that you have to learn it and play it through your senses. You must be mindful but not thoughtful as you swing. You must not think or reflect. You must feel what you have to do. Part of the difficulty arises because, apart from some things like riding a bike, we have never learned to do things in this way."[5]

We have heard good golfers say they do not think about the swing when playing. They truly do not. They are playing by feel. Lots of things we do in our everyday life we do by FEEL or MUSCLE MEMORY. We do things without thinking "How To." You cannot think about "How To" to get your swing to repeat under pressure. But you can try and make the swing FEEL the same way all the time. REMEMBER what the swing feels like, and repeat that Feel, not the "How To."

"Please note that Walter Hagen did not concentrate in the accepted sense. Walter had found, by trial and error as most of us do, how he could best hit the ball. He had gotten the FEEL of his shots thoroughly into his system and could pull them out whenever he wanted."[6]

The "How To" in golf is very important, but only to a point. You must start to feel what the "How To" feels like if you are going to repeat your swing. When you hit a shot, good or bad, the individual characteristics of what you feel must be recognized. If your goal is to have a golf swing that can respond to what has been called "MUSCLE MEMORY," please accept that you should not be trying to MEMORIZE "How To."

TRUE PROGRESS, to play better golf with consistency, comes only when the "How To" in golf is joined with FEEL. When the FEEL of the SWING starts to become more important, than "How To," you have started to achieve TRUE PROGRESS.

"The golf swing is a CONNECTED SERIES of sensations or feels, and when you get all these feels right and rightly connected, you will swing perfectly."[7]

We have all seen athletes in all sports go through some sort of pre-performance routine. Then, when all is about to start, they walk away and start all over. The reason they walked away was they did not FEEL right. They are very good at what they do, but they have to FEEL it before they can do it. Baseball players are always starting over after they appear to be set. All of us in our everyday life, after we start to be good at one thing or another, will say, "I have the feel of it (or the "Muscle Memory") to do it again." We have all said it. We have all done it. So how do you think you did it? You remember what it feels like, and then repeat the feel, not the "How To."

When a good golfer is standing over a shot, he is trying to repeat the feel of the address position, not do this or do that. When the swing starts, he is trying to feel the movement. As the swing moves to the top of the backswing, he FEELS something. That tells him it is time to go forward.

Expert golfers, both professional and amateur, have filled out questionnaires on what they FEEL when playing. (Not how they play). We are going to use these answers to help define what you are FEELING in your golf game, and give you new tools to make progress.

"No teacher can tell in exact words how it feels when you make a certain movement correctly. You will have to use your own imagination - and if he is wise he will encourage you to do so."[8]

Golf attracts new players every day because it looks like fun and it is not too hard to play. Most books will state that it is not too hard to play. Also, any golfer who has a nice game will tell you that golf is not all that hard. The truth is, if you follow a few fundamentals and practice, things can fall into place for your game. When you read what good players feel when playing, you will have another tool to learn with.

Because no two golfers would feel the swing the same way, this section may confuse you. But if you have never paid attention to the feel of your swing, it's time you did. It is a key that could help you in repeating your swing. It is the right hemisphere at work! Listed on the following pages are statements from some leading golfers about feel, followed by answers to the questionnaire. Use the answers, not as guidelines to what you should be feeling, but as tools to help you in defining your own feel.

5, 6, 7, 8 - Percy Boomer

BOBBY JONES: "The primary aim in teaching must be to *communicate* to the golfer the feel of making a proper golf stroke."

BEN HOGAN: "I am an *advocate* of the kind of *teaching* which stresses the exact nature and feel of the movements a player makes to achieve the results he wants."

ARNOLD PALMER: "The swing is largely a matter of feel."

GARY PLAYER: "There is a definite 'feeling,' and this feeling is to be DEVELOPED AND LOOKED FOR."

JACK NICKLAUS: "I'll try to 'feel' the shot, GENERALLY, RATHER THAN SPECIFICALLY, then swing before I lose the feel."

JOHNNY MILLER: "The GOLF SWING is built largely on MUSCLE MEMORY."

BEN HOGAN: "The more a golfer can trust his swing to muscle memory (feel), the more attention he can then turn to managing his game."

JACK NICKLAUS: "Another point about swing 'SYMMETRY.' Get it out of your head. You should feel you are making the same basic swing with every club."

BEN HOGAN: "A good golfer acquires feel and rhythm through practice."

JACK NICKLAUS: "In practice I am developing FEEL."

JACK NICKLAUS: "To me, once your mechanics are reasonably sound, FEEL becomes the CRITICAL FACTOR."

SURVEY

DO YOU HAVE ANY THOUGHTS ABOUT FEEL?

M.T.   I believe golf is all feel, that's why good players can lay off for months and come right back to winning forms.

M.T.   Feel should be more a part of instruction than it currently is - it is what separates the "players" from the mechanical players.

L.T.   I believe it can be taught and that it varies from day to day - some days you can feel certain "keys" better; other days it may have to be more mechanical.

L.T.   The only way by which one should strive to play the game. By "feeling" the movements - good or bad - one can then correct or maintain them. *Playing* the game by "feel," one allows the subconscious mind to do its job of swinging the club. *Practicing* by "feel" is the most effective way the conscious mind will tell (teach) the subconscious proper swing positions. Proper *visualization* is essential as well and works to promote proper feel.

L.T.   It is the one thing that takes the golfer from the good ranks to the professional or great player ranks. This is because not all shots are meant to be full shots. If you hit a five iron 155 yards - what do you do if you have 148-158 yards to the pin? . . . OR a 35 foot putt or slow Bermuda Greens versus fast bent?

M.T.   Yes, definitely - you must feel the shot in advance pinpointing your feel at contact and working toward a balanced firm finish!

T.P.   Feel is an important part of the game. But it is only developed through the constant practice of the fundamantals.

M.T.   I think it is the most important part of advancing in teaching a pupil. Once he can get some feeling of what he is trying to do then you are on your way to helping and improving him - NO FEEL - NO PLAYER - there are a lot of bad swingers, but great players are "great" because they have a feeling of club - muscles, rhythm, etc. I have never met or talked to good players who are not always talking and using the word feel in describing or EXPLAINING types of shots and swings.

L.T.   To me "feel" is the key to the whole game:
1) Helps tempo
2) Is the key for hitting the shot pin high. Hitting the shot on line every time is exceptional, but the player hitting the shot pin high every time to me plays with topic, "feel." So, the player, especially the beginner and the high handicapper, should work harder on judging how far the shot is, they would score better if they knew their distances better.
   Great players that play with feel for distance: Boros, Trevino, Casper, Littler, Bolt. They don't have to walk off the distance - they take a look and hit. Maybe this is a gift that we don't all have. One thing they do have in common is "feel."

IN TERMS OF FEEL
WHAT DOES YOUR ADDRESS FEEL LIKE?

M.T.   Relaxed, but taut left side.

M.T.   Comfortable and not contrived - muscles ready to respond.

L.T.   Feels like my left side is a little higher - kind of like I'm ready to wind up from the feet UP!

L.T.   I feel parallel with shoulders, hips, feet and line of flight. I feel club face square to imaginary line of flight in my mind.

L.T.   After a basic address position is established for myself through practice and observation, I just try to repeat this by repetition and comfort is the most important feel.

M.T.   Comfortable on balance with most of weight on left side.

T.P.   More weight on the right side enables me to pull my left knee behind the ball.

M.T.   My address feeling is of proper width of feet, with a good solid distribution of weight from heel to toes, and a continuous feeling of *movement* and *rhythm-shifting*.

L.T.   1) Depending upon shot being played. 2) My weight distribution is what I feel - more to the left on shorter shots, etc.

L.T.   Feel right side (shoulder-hip-arm) hangs from my left. 75% of my weight is on my right foot - ball of foot to heel.

L.T.   My best address position - balance; muscle set; steadiness and solidity over ball; comfortable; effortless; no excess motion; fluidness possible in preparing for swing.

M.T.   Shoulders and hips just left of target - feet at target or just right - weight on inside of feet (balls of feet) - legs braced against each other.

M.T.   My arms are hanging naturally. I feel as if I have a little more weight on the inside of my right foot. My knees are slightly flexed and a slight bend from the waist. My shoulders feel "wide," not hunched.

T.P.   I feel I am well balanced and there isn't any tension in my body.

M.T.   I feel comfortable or relaxed in my legs, arms hang freely approximately six to nine inches away from stomach. Stance is slightly open. Legs are slightly flexed.

M.T.   At address, I feel very relaxed in the bottom of my feet - I'm ready to spring straight up. I feel like a Quarterback in position behind a center.

T.P.   Comfortable, with as much tension taken out of the right side as possible.

T.P.   I feel an upward feeling through my body but a hanging feeling from the shoulders.

T.P.   Comfortable - usually soft, alert, getting a preliminary feel of what the ball will do!

T.P.   I try to feel as upright as possible. Not stiff but tall. My knees flexed but not locked.

M.T.   I stand as close to the ball as possible. I feel solid in my thighs and lower back because of sit down type position.

WHAT DO YOU FEEL WHEN YOU HOLD THE CLUB?

M.T.   Equal Pressure in both hands.

M.T.   Both hands feel as one - firmness without tension.

L.T.   Firmness up left arm and in last three fingers of left hand - feel of the leather on the grip in the fingers of my right hand.

L.T.   Hands felt to work like a "unit" - firm pressure from both hands - yet a softness to the touch.

L.T.   Just try to maintain enough pressure to grip the club with control.

M.T.   Club head mostly. Try to feel all of the club, predominantly the club head.

T.P.   Get your arms feeling really light so that you can feel club head.

M.T.   That the club must feel in its proper position in my hands - more in *palm* and (*muscle-pad*) feeling of my left hand with definite finger feeling in the right hand. STRESS ON PRESSURE POINTS - OF MY GRIP.

L.T.   1) Size of grip
        2) Stiffness of shaft
        3) Head weight

L.T.   Try to make my hands comfortable - have even grip pressure at all points of contact between grip of club and hands.

L.T.   Different things - more than one gets good results. Varying feelings of: calmness; hands telling me direction of swing; relaxation but not necessarily looseness; sometimes awkwardness if forcing hands to make a change; awareness of weight of club and balance of club; familiarity of a club I've seen many times.

M.T.   Get hands to feel as one unit - helps to get left thumb directly down middle of grip.

M.T.   I feel greater grip pressure in my left hand, preferably in the last three fingers. My right side is a bit more passive than the left.

M.T.   Don't know.

T.P.   I feel the club is not too light or heavy for me. My grip is correct and I am not holding the club too tight.

M.T.   I feel pressure in the last three fingers of my left hand and two middle fingers on my right. This pressure is only firm enough to hold on to the club.

M.T.   I feel the handle, then I lift the head a little off the ground so I can feel the head.

T.P.   The pressure feels light but the left hand feels in control.

T.P.   Unity in the two hands and a feel for the overall club.

M.T.   Depends on the shot!
        1) Sometimes a light "neutral" feeling in the hands (both hands as one); 2) Sometimes a "lock" with left hand; and right hand light; 3) Sometimes a loose "fingery" feel.

WHAT DO YOU FEEL DURING BACKSWING?

M.T.   Good long left arm extension; winding of the lower back muscles.

M.T.   Shoulders moving club away - coiling - attempting to feel club behind me.

L.T.   I feel my feet more during my swing than anything else - my left foot rolls inward as the club starts away from the ball - and the backswing just winds up.

L.T.   A smoothness, and coiling.

M.T.   Upper torso turning with hands going up staying under the club.

M.T.   Moving into it smoothly from my address position set-up with concentration of turning and staying over the ball.

L.T.   1) Shoulder turn.
       2) A "set position" at top - I feel something with my wrists at top.

M.T.   Whole left side coils against braced right side.

M.T.   I feel my arms "swing" back as a result of a good shoulder turn. As my shoulders turn, my hips turn until I feel my left knee behind the ball. I like to feel as if I pause at the top.

M.T.   Turning right hip level.

M.T.   I try to feel tempo or smoothness. I do not want to be quick, extension back away from the ball.

M.T.   Patience, and I feel strength gathering in my body during the backswing.

T.P.   A windup of the left side around the trunk of the body.

M.T.   1) When swinging well - an absence of any tension.

       2) When not swinging well - an awareness of tension to be consciously overcome!

T.P.   A gradual feeling of increasing tightness as the backswing progresses. Less tightness for a short shot. Mostly tension not grip tension.

M.T.   I try to have no feel except left side domination, as slow as possible. I also try to avoid any sudden moves at top.

T.P.   I feel my body coil up behind the ball and my left arm feels completely straight.

M.T.   I am feeling target conscious. That must come to mind.

L.T.   Very little. It's mental for me. I have a picture in my mind of what I want to do and when I feel I am in the proper position I automatically just let my swing happen.

L.T.   I "feel" a coiling of my whole body without knowing where the club is.

M.T.   I have the feeling of smoothness, acceleration and balance.

T.P.   A coiling of the left side against the right leg. I feel my whole backswing as a movement of my left shoulder under my chin.

T.P.   My body coiling - but only for a split second.

WHAT DO YOU FEEL DURING FORWARD SWING?

M.T.   Lower left leading with free arm swing - head stays in position.

L.T.   I feel a thrust across my right foot as my left arm starts back down - I feel rhythm from my feet up my legs.

L.T.   I "feel" the line of flight and a smooth unwinding, yet much accelerated from the backswing. Solid contact.

L.T.   I feel that I just reverse the series of the backswing with the feeling that I am applying more pull on the forward swing than on the take away.

M.T.   Weight return to left side, hands ahead of club using club as late as possible and a rotation of the body after contact.

M.T.   The continuation of the total swing that got you to the top of the backswing, and now feeling like coming into the forward swing by "rocking" or shifting laterally to my left side.

L.T.   Total move to finish; completion of visual image of hit at ball; balance in motion; "feel" things relative to mechanical things I'm working on; in good swings effortlessness.

M.T.   Legs reverse swing - right hip fires through ball toward target.

M.T.   I feel I initiate the forward swing by replanting the left heel and "pulling" with my left side. Sometimes I feel as if I push off the inside of my right foot.

M.T.   Staying behind the ball.

T.P.   The smooth shifting of the body to the left side.

M.T.   Patience and quietness in my change of direction - then I feel the impulse of energy I built in my backswing release.

T.P.   An unwinding of the muscles that were coiled on the backswing.

T.P.   I feel my lower body spins very fast and my hands whip through.

M.T.   Acceleration and release of the club down the target line.

T.P.   A release of the tightness by starting with my legs first.

M.T.   I try to feel a strong drive with knees and legs to move to left side before impact. Left hip to clear.

T.P.   I feel my legs driving at the ball in a flexed position and my left arm feels like it returns to the ball in a straight rigid position.

M.T.   All thoughts are at the flag, it's hard to feel anything but the club going through.

L.T.   I feel POWER, being generated, ever increasing, through and past the hitting area.

L.T.   I "feel" a tremendous burst of energy and a throwing action - all in a super short moment.

DO YOU HAVE ANY SPECIAL FEELING
AT THE END OF YOUR SWING?

M.T.   Not really.

M.T.   Balance and freedom.

L.T.   I feel totally released across and through to the left side with my weight rolled over on outside of left foot slightly.

L.T.   Balance. A rocking back on right side once shot is underway. Relaxation.

L.T.   Relaxation still with firm grip on club in a balanced mode.

T.P.   A spent feeling at the end of my swing.

M.T.   Not so much - think more of hitting area and releasing there! End of swing doesn't matter, it is over with by then.

L.T.   If it has been a good swing, I feel relaxed except - I fight to keep my hands or arms from folding over my shoulder - never allow right hip or right shoulder to rise above left hip or shoulder - when this position feels uncomfortable - I walk away.

L.T.   Balance; good swing feels like nothing happened.

M.T.   Balanced - could pick up right foot - 90% weight on left leg.

M.T.   I like to feel as if I've really extended through the shot and finish high.

M.T.   Reaching for the sky.

T.P.   That the feeling of the swing has been completed with very little effort.

M.T.   Balance and hands high.

T.P.   No, other than a feeling of good balance on the shots where everything occurred in the proper sequence.

T.P.   I like to have an around type of feeling with the weight on the left side.

M.T.   1) When swinging well - balance and controlled force.
2) When not swinging well - anticipation and anxiety.

T.P.   That my body still occupies the same place at the finish that it did at the start and my left knee is still flexed. I feel completely unwound.

M.T.   Just to finish in as balanced a position as possible.

T.P.   I have a feeling of being stretched down the line of the shot with the club ending up in a high position to the left of the line.

M.T.   I feel I've completed my swing best when my head is brought up by the momentum of the follow through. ONLY never *forcing* myself to watch the ball go down the fairway.

M.T.   I like to feel balanced. If the shot is good I feel good. If the shot is bad I feel bad.

M.T.   Relaxation.

DURING THE SWING, IS YOUR HEAD PART OF THE TOTAL FEEL, OR IS THERE A SPECIAL FEEL FOR THE HEAD!

M.T.　　Part of the total feel, I try to keep it up on the backswing.

M.T.　　Part of the total feel.

L.T.　　My head feels like it stays behind the ball throughout my swing, but other than that I don't think about it or feel it.

L.T.　　Part of total feel. It feels free to move (rotate). Relaxed neck muscles.

L.T.　　It does its own thing as far as allowing the body to swing around itself and remain behind the ball until impact.

M.T.　　Try not to move head by keeping eyes focused on ball through impact then head goes with clubhead.

T.P.　　My head is stationary - my body is detached and separate from head.

M.T.　　I like it to feel relaxed in neck and natural - but try to keep it as still as I can.

L.T.　　No, has nothing to do with my feel during the swing.

L.T.　　On the downswing of a good swing I feel my head stays way behind the ball - actually my main two thoughts are head behind legs through.

L.T.　　Head would be part of feel if working on position; however, I associate more visual images to my head.

M.T.　　Head attached to spine - spine moves in swing so the head must move too.

M.T.　　During impact I feel like my head is behind the ball. I try to keep it as steady as possible in my total swing.

M.T.　　Rock steady.

T.P.　　Your head is separate from the rest of your body. You should feel it is on a pedestal.

M.T.　　The head should stay as I can keep it. The head can move off the ball and back on to the ball.

M.T.　　I try to keep my head high and feel the rest of my body working beneath my head.

T.P.　　Part of the total, although the central part.

T.P.　　I don't think much about the head, however, I must admit I did a lot in practice.

M.T.　　Sometimes the head is used as the hub! Most times it follows the action of the swing naturally. Playing well there is almost no *strain* in the neck.

T.P.　　I feel as though my head is the center of the swing and everything revolves around it.

DO YOU FEEL ANY DIFFERENT
WHEN PLAYING SHORT GAME SHOTS?

M.T.   More precise, more stable, more solid, more left side oriented.

M.T.   The shorter the shot - the less motion used - feel is basically same.

L.T.   I don't feel as *much* in my feet - but feel the distance for 50 - 70 yard shots more with my left arm and shoulder - feel my hands more on shorter shots - maneuver the clubhead with hands.

L.T.   Firmer - more definite stroking motion. My whole feeling is concentrated on line of shot.

L.T.   Yes - the short shots are "feel" in that there is no set swing for easy shots - you and your mind with reference to your reflexes determine how far you move the ball. You have to "feel" the distance rather than the swing.

M.T.   No - short swing is just a segment of long swing.

T.P.   More weight on left side during address.

M.T.   Very definitely! Like a *softer* but *firm* grip and even change my grip on shorter shots at times because I want a special feel for special shots.

L.T.   Yes, in my set up I feel a change of weight distribution - everything else the same.

L.T.   Yes - each situation presents different requirements - after deciding what shot is called for I rely on memory of the feel I had of a successful shot that was similar to the one called for. Only constant is feel of head staying still.

L.T.   Yes. Same qualities in a different form.

M.T.   Yes, my arms "feel" softer. I relax my grip when playing shots that require a lot of "feel."

M.T.   Yes - total looseness.

T.P.   Yes, I feel the shot with my hands.

M.T.   I try to exaggerate tempo. Keep it slow and accelerate the club through impact.

M.T.   I feel less energy build on my backswing.

T.P.   The overall feel is lighter and slower.

T.P.   I just try to have control of the club early in the swing.

M.T.   Softer; quieter - feelings are mostly mental and I make a big effort to encourage positive feelings.

T.P.   No, it's just a "mini" swing. Less wrist action because the swing doesn't progress as far.

M.T.   I try to feel the distance. I grip lighter to aid my touch.

T.P.   I only feel a shorter distance that the club travels.

Part IV

- *Coaching Suggestions*

- *Research*

- *Other Thoughts*

- *Balance*

- *Force*

- *Flat Spot*

I have been asked many times, "What is involved in making progress as a player or coach"? My answer has always been the same, "I am not sure I know the whole answer, but in part it will take time, money, and help."

Good players and coaches have *no* secrets. What they do have is an uncomplicated and simple approach to the golf swing that is based on the laws of motion. This section will get some insight and understanding to *why* things happen the way they do in a sound swing.

Our approach to coaching is based on the laws of physics and motion. In this section of the book there is a summary of golf swing research that I feel will be very helpful in understanding the golf swing. It gives the reader the Scientific Reasons or Scientific Foundation for our approach.

The Time: In my case, I spend 40 to 50 hours a week teaching and another 10 to 15 hours on research and study.

The Money: Over the years more than $25,000 has been spent on cameras; developing film; books; teaching aids; video equipment; traveling to tournaments to study players; video tapes; etc.

The Help: No one coach has enough *time* or the *ability* to learn and gather all the information that is needed. Help from others (their discoveries, their failures, their research) is necessary.

When reading someone else's books or research, keep in mind that in just a few hours we are exposed to information and knowledge that has taken many years for its author to gather. Progress, in any learning process, is because of team work. Adding to your point of view, the discoveries others have made is the necessary step all successful coaches have made.

I would like to strongly recommend the books, *The Search for the Perfect Swing* Cochran and Stobbs, *30 Exercises For Better Golf* by Frank Jobe, and *Exercise Fitness For Golf* by the National Golf Foundation.

There is only a short summary of these works in this section of the book. To have the fullest understanding of the golf swing (the how and why), you must add these books to your own library.

COACHING AND TEACHING SUGGESTIONS

Where should we start?
What should we start with?
Are some things more important than others?

Ken Venturi said, "No one will ever convince me the most important element of the golf swing is not the POSITION of the body at address, a good starting position."

Jack Nicklaus told us, "Hitting good golf shots - 50% mental, 40% set up, 10% swing."

Dave Pelz points out, "Over 60% of our golf swings are from 60 yards or closer to the hole in a round."

We all know "After we learn how to hit the ball, we still have to learn how to play."

Dave Pelz tells us, "Physical Talent is important, but is truly insignificant in comparison to the mental aspect of learning."

Mike Hebron "One can help someone to learn and reach potential but one really cannot teach a physical skill; students teach themselves."

Any of the above statements could be used as a suggestion on *where* golf instruction could start and *what* could be covered at that point. Where any type of instruction starts is very important, but there is some latitude as to the exact *where* or *what*. Before moving on it may be important and helpful to answer a question; "How IMPORTANT is teaching and coaching golf?"

- When a coach or a professional has the opportunity to make someone's leisure time more enjoyable,
   That's Important!

- When a coach or a professional has the opportunity to introduce a game to a young person that he/she can enjoy for the rest of his/her lifetime,
   That's Important!

- When a coach or a professional has the opportunity to give a family a common interest, so that they can spend time together,
   That's Important!

- When a coach or a professional introduces an activity to a retired person so that it can be a form of exercise and companionship,
   That's Important!

- When a coach or a professional has the opportunity to bring a game to a young person so that it will put him/her in the company of adults on a somewhat equal basis,
   That's Important!

Golf can be many things: *Companionship, Exercise, Competition,* a *Challenge* to your learning skills, *Enjoyment* of the great outdoors, and much more. As you develop your teaching and coaching skills, you will nurture an important tool that will enable you to reach and touch far beyond that which most of us can imagine today. In my view, both the coach and PGA Professional have an obligation to strengthen this important tool. (Teaching, Coaching, and Promoting Golf are the most important responsibilities a PGA professional has.) My hope is that the following information will give you some useful ideas so that you can add to those you already have and use.

So, what is the first step in giving a golf lesson? Is the answer somewhere on the previous pages or is the answer so obvious it could be easily overlooked? The answer is,

YOU HAVE TO BE ASKED!

Yes, someone has to request that you give him/her a lesson. You will only be asked if you have given the impression that you are capable of helping improve his/her golf game. Thus, the first step towards giving golf instruction will be based upon your image and credibility.

There are many ways to build image and credibility: be a member of a professional organization; graduate from college; use the latest tools of your profession; to have letters or recommendation and/or awards; to be honest, fair, and reliable; to be professional; personal appearance, just to mention a few.

Perhaps you have had little time to attain some of the things mentioned to help with your image and credibility, but you can always act in a professional manner. You can be honest, fair, reliable, and always make a personal appearance that is professional and business-like. You can use some teaching tools of your profession. At first, these teaching aids do not have to be of the latest design, but having them will add to your image and your credibility. That is most important.

A weighted club, inexpensive Polaroid camera, after-lesson suggestion pad, some teaching pictures to show students, rope, a big mirror, spray paint, umbrella, broom, tennis balls, short clubs, 2 x 4 pieces of wood, all can be used and will not take a big investment on your part to have available when coaching.

All coaches will have their favorite teaching aids. When you start to coach you have but a few, nevertheless they are important. Ideas and suggestions from other professionals will help you to add to your inventory of teaching aids.

Before a lesson starts or a new golf season gets under way, let's ask, "Why do some golfers make faster progress than others?" Your answer at times may be, "Some golfers are better students than others!" *Some* students overlook that they have a responsibility that must be met if they want to see progress.

As a coach, you may wish to spend some time explaining and showing students how to benefit best from lesson experience, the *Before, During,* and *After.* If you are working with a student who does not understand this process, it is certain the student's progress will be slow.

Before a lesson starts, students should know what to expect. Students should have an understanding of what will occur during a lesson, and some background information on who will be giving it. *During* the lesson, you, as the coach, must explain to the student the reason for your suggestions and instructions for change. Then, *After* a lesson students must realize that what they do between lessons can be more important than their next lesson. Students must spend time and effort with the suggestions made during a lesson. Stress practice.

Now on with the lesson. It will be very helpful before a coach gives any suggestions that he/she has some knowledge of what a student thinks about when making a swing. How would the student explain the swing? How is the student trying to swing? Ask your student those questions. For me, this is the starting point, the first step, and a must before I can be of any help to a student. At times students say one thing and do something else. A coach has to know what the student is thinking about, even if the answer is "Nothing."

Most golf coaches would tell us that when they first gave lessons they "over taught." Try your best to avoid over teaching. Keep in mind a big part of progress is self-discovery. Let the students know you are acting in their best interests when you cover one maybe two points during a lesson. They must learn; to cover more than that would take away from the value of the lesson.

After the student understands your suggestions, he/she must get the feel of the movements you would like to see. Getting the feel is going to take some time and self discovery. This is where I think students are really teaching themselves with the help of a coach. When coaching, try to get students to remember the feel of what they are doing: the feel of the correct grip and posture, the feel of the backswing, the feel of a chip shot and the feel of a putt. I could go on, but try and have students become aware of what they are feeling when playing.

Each student may describe this feeling differently, but for him/her to be aware that the good and the bad swings feel different is very important in the learning process. When you do some reading and research (and you should) about golf, you are going to find "feel" is written and talked about as much, if not more, than any other aspect of the golf swing.

Jack Nicklaus told us. "I work on feel, to me once your mechanics are reasonable, feel is the critical factor"; "Feel out your shots with your practice swing"; "The down swing happens too quickly to be consciously directed, it's much more a matter of feel"; "In my own case, I'll employ feel as I plan the swing." One could fill several books with all the short and small quotes I have come across over the years about "feel."

During the lesson it's important to find something positive to say about every swing before you then make a constructive comment on it. THIS IS MOST IMPORTANT! No matter how new the golfer may be, or how much improvement you may feel his/her style needs, there is always something positive a coach could mention followed by your observations for improvement.

EXAMPLE: "Mr. Green, I liked your tempo during that swing. You did not jump away at the start and you were nice and smooth with your front swing. It may be helpful if on the next swing you make more of a weight transfer on the way back. This will give the swing the kind of weight transfer we are looking for on the front swing. It is hard to have an acceptable weight transfer going forward if we do not have one going back, but I loved the tempo and speed of the swing. That's what we are looking for."

You can and must find something positive about every swing on which you comment. When you do, your students will become more coachable and willing to work and learn.

Let students know that even though they cannot see any progress, you as the coach can. They cannot see themselves swing; they can only see what the ball is doing. Students are going to be much harder on themselves than a skilled coach would be. A coach can see the grip improving; a coach can see the legs of the student starting to do their part; a coach can see the weight transfer starting to become a natural part of the swing. Letting students know that you can see progress and improvement is very important to the learning process. Keep in mind that students cannot see themselves and are only aware of what the ball is doing.

It has been said that a golf coach needs a lot of patience, I would disagree. I know I do not have a lot of patience and in one of Percy Boomer's books he told us he did not have much either. What a skilled coach may have is a realistic idea of what to expect from students and how long it is going to take before a noticeable change will occur.

When watching a skilled coach give a lesson and the student has yet to send a ball on its way with reasonable flight and distance, (missing the ball more often than not), you may say, "How can this coach spend so much time and interest with such a duff; he will run short of patience soon." WRONG! We overlook that the coach often knows the kind of shot a student will make before the swing takes place, and is making suggestions so the student will eventually see progress. It is not PATIENCE you are observing when you see a skilled coach at work, but realistic understanding of the LEARNING PROCESS.

When someone first comes to you for a lesson, there is a very good chance the student has already taken some lessons elsewhere. You must keep this in mind, and ask about them. Find out what was covered in these sessions. What did other coaches explain and feel was important. Do not, under any circumstances, express fault about other coaches or their information. Nothing is to be gained by this except a loss of your own credibility with a new student.

If you are uncomfortable with the instructions a student is receiving from another coach, find a way to say you would like to try a different approach. Be prepared to explain "why" you want the student to work with your suggestions.

"Why" as it pertains to the fundamentals of the swing.

"Why" as it pertains to the student's style as you see it on the day of the lesson.

"Why" as it pertains to the progress you would like to see for the student.

Letting the student know that golf can only be learned in steps and stages is going to be helpful to both of you. As a coach, you may want to make several suggestions to students after watching them practice. Let the students know there are several suggestions you could make that would make their golf more enjoyable. But in fairness to you as a coach and to them as students, only one or maybe two things can be worked on at a time.

Make the students aware that they will not see progress until they work — that no one has ever improved without expending time and effort. Again, you are doing the students and yourself, as the coach, a service when they fully understand that it takes time before they will see progress or change.

Studies tell us it takes 17 days to learn a new habit, and 45 days to replace an old habit with a new one. When students are aware of the time and effort needed, they put less pressure on themselves.

In your approach to a lesson let students know that a coach (in a sense) does not teach them to play golf. Students teach themselves with some help from a coach. Learning golf is like learning to draw, play music, or drive a car. When learning these skills, students have really taught themselves. This is unlike being taught Math, English, or History, in which the teacher is providing all information needed for a student's progress. In golf, "Information comes from a coach, skill from the student." (Bill Strausbaugh) If a student is to see progress it's the teamwork between the two of you that will open the door to better golf.

At the start of the lesson, it would be helpful to have the students give you some information about their past golf experiences and what they expect to achieve. Many students are not at ease during a lesson, especially at its beginning. Tell them a lesson is not a "TEST."; that you are not concerned about how or where the ball is going during your time together; that they are spending time with you to receive some suggestions to be used in the future.

Find ways to put students at ease. There is a fine line between "Attention" and "Tension." You must be aware *when* the student crosses that line. One must pay attention in golf, but any mental or physical tension will create a road block in anyone's progress. Tight body or grip, quick movements, lack of balance, are all generally caused by tension.

Tension often comes from a lack of "Trust." The club can be held lighter and the body relaxed far more so than most students will first trust or believe. A coach must get students to "trust." Students must be encouraged to believe in what you are asking them to execute. Let students know their golf will greatly improve when they *"trust"* and expend *"time"* and *"effort."*

Pay attention, keep it simple, do not mistake *Intentions* for *Attention*, is the message that will help students. An example of Good Intentions; "I just want to hit the ball and play better." This type of thinking is not as helpful to a golfer as paying *Attention* to the fundamentals he/she has learned. "I want to be a better golfer"; that's good *Intentions* and is easily mistaken for *Attention!*

Visualization can be the first step away from tension. Teach your students how to see the ball in flight before they swing: to see the ball hitting the green; to see the ball going in the hole; to always see and visualize a positive result; to visualize where the ball should go. *Do Not* visualize where you do not want the ball to go. *Never* say "I do not want to be in the water or trap or O.B." This would be the first step away from *Attention*, and a step in the direction of *Tension.*

In golf, mistakes are made; they just don't happen! When students understand this, they will be more relaxed and attentive to your suggestions. There are reasons (cause and effect) for a sound swing. When your students learn the reasons for sound swings, they will not say, "Why did that happen?" after a shot, good or bad, they will know.

Golf is played with the nervous system. Conditions and surroundings often cause the golf swing to change. We have all heard, "On the range I hit the ball super, but I never hit a good one off the 1st tee," or "I never play well when I play with my husband." Both student and coach must realize "The mind does not hit the ball, but it can stop the swing." *(Dave Pelz)*

A coach should be aware that it is very difficult for most students to make a good golf swing when the previous one was poor. This would be like telling a joke that did not get a laugh the first time we told it. Most of us would not retell the joke, but in golf we must make the next swing.

Teach students how to train their minds. "To change on the inside first, then work on the outside. The body cannot learn, only the mind can. Physical talent is important, but it is truly insignificant in comparison to the mental aspect of learning." *(Dave Pelz)*

As a coach you should acquire all the knowledge you can about the mental aspect of learning. It is likely you will not reach your potential as a coach until you make progress in this subject.

A coach is going to find it helpful if the words he/she chooses to use in a lesson can be turned into pictures or visualization. When it comes to this, some words are better than others. For example, if a coach were to use the word "SLOW," it may not be as useful as the phrase "5 Mph." When asking students to define SLOW, there is a good chance each answer will be very different and dissimilar from the next. On the other hand, when asking to define "5 Mph," you may find the answer is more alike. "5 Mph" will mean the same to almost everyone whereas the word "SLOW" will have a much broader meaning. Again, my suggestion is to use words and phrases that can be turned into visualizations. We very rarely forget someone's face, but it's very easy to forget names. A face is a picture in your mind, a name is a word in the mind that is forgotten sooner than a picture.

Until a coach and the student can recognize the same swing there will be little progress. The two of you must work as a team. If you, as a coach, use the word "Back," your student has to be applying the same meaning as you do. This is essential. Information, both verbal and visual, should be traveling back and forth between coach and student at all times. Do not make a student just a target for your suggestions. "That would be Preaching, not Teaching."

Teaching, Coaching and Learning is Teamwork. It is said that good teams start to think alike. This should be the goal of a golf coach and student. This will not happen overnight. It will take time, but you must reach for it — that common ground and understanding from which a student's golf game can grow.

The coach will have to work much harder than the student if this goal is to be attained. A coach must have a set pattern of ideas he/she feels will lead to student progress. However, all students will be quite different, one from the other. Because of this, a coach will require many different ways to share his/her experiences. (Many different ways!) A skilled coach always has to be prepared for the student who will want to take over the lesson — the type of student who wants to do the talking, do the teaching, do the showing. An excellent way to approach this kind of student is to listen patiently, but from time to time just comment, "Try this, and let's see what happens." Your obligation as a professional coach is to help students. Whether the students feel the coach helped or they helped themselves is really unimportant.

New golfers watch others who have been playing longer. They may also watch professionals, either in person or on T.V. New golfers are not alone in this activity. All golfers, at every level, watch other golfers. I think for the most part, it can be very helpful to watch others play. This is how we first learned to do things as children — by looking and imitating.

In golf, we must learn to recognize the difference between personal mannerisms and the actions of a sound swing. It can be very easy to be misled by what we think we see when looking at a golf swing. As a coach, help your students learn how to look at a golfer and gain useful information.

Teach students to see, feel, and admire balance, posture, and the slow change of direction. Teach them to see and feel the ball in the way of the swing, to note a lack of quick-jerk type movement, and to look for swing finish. If you do not, students will recognize and search for strength, power, speed, hit, distance, and never realize golf is a game played in the "state of grace."

A coach should impress upon a student that his/her body never moves on its own. Movement happens for one of three reasons: (1) *Reflexes*, when something moves and the body reacts to that movement. (2) *Anticipation*, when one makes one's body move before other movement happens. A defensive team will anticipate where the next offensive play will occur. (3) The last reason one's body moves is when one's mind tells the body what to do. Taking a foul shot in basketball or bowling or making a golf swing are all examples of movements that have *not* been caused by reflexes or anticipation. In these cases, the mind sent a message through the nervous system to the muscular system telling the body what to do.

Keep in mind, the message your mind sends can only be based on the kind of information stored in the brain. As a coach, you have to help students store useful golf information in the mind's eye, to encourage students to exchange *helpful concepts* for poor ones. Without question, the most important keys in golf are the *concepts* and *visualization* of the swing that are stored in the mind's eye.

A coach must learn the difference between the right and left side of the brain. Both have different responsibilities. The right side works with pictures, feelings, concepts, while the left with words. It is very important to learn about this subject. You *will not* reach your potential as a coach until you do. You will certainly discover pictures are more important than words when teaching or learning a physical skill.

One of the reasons people do not play the standard of golf they seek is because they don't play enough. Give them the following example and you may find they will have a more realistic understanding why progress in golf takes time. In a round where the score of 100 was made, let's say 36 putts and 14 chip shots were taken, leaving just 50 full swings. Fifty swings are a pail of balls at a driving range. The balls take 20-30 minutes to hit. Actually, it takes only a few seconds to put a ball in place and then swing. So in reality a pail of balls only produces 4 or 5 minutes of swing-time. One is on the course for *several hours* to enjoy just *4 or 5 minutes of swing time.* You can imagine someone typing 4 or 5 minutes each day trying to learn to type! The point is we must tell students it's swing time that counts, not the number of days, weeks, or years they play. No one spends long stretches of time (or swing time) on golf, thus, it is this one reason golfers do not play up to their expectations.

As a coach, you must take into consideration that most students' self-image will have an influence on their standard of play and the progress they make. Students generally feel they should be scoring better than they achieve because of the rounds and years they have been playing. It is your responsibility to clearly explain how much golf they *really* have played, and, as a skilled coach, that you feel they are making progress. Build confidence!

You will not be a successful coach unless you like and respect people. To have some knowledge of the golf swing and the game is but a very small part a skilled coach must master. When someone asks for your help and is going to pay for your time and information, you must treat that person as a "tour star." Pay attention to the person's needs both as an individual and golfer. Consider weaknesses as carefully as strengths. Encourage students to become excited about their new learning experiences. Show and explain that progress is being made; golf is fun when making a score of 95 to 100, even more fun with scores of 85 to 90. Tell them that poor shots and swings are part of the learning process.

As a coach, you should point out to your student that golfers are always receiving tips from friends and other golfers. Inform students that accepting this kind of information will only slow progress. Encourage a student who enjoys reading about golf and its mechanics, to discuss the reading with you. Discussion with you will help the student.

Some closing thoughts: (I didn't use the words "Final Thoughts" because when it comes to teaching and coaching there are none. There is always more to come; new and different ways to help golfers get more enjoyment out of the game we all love.)

"The" Perfect Swing does not exist — but "A" Perfect Swing does. Your goal, as a coach, should be to help your students find "A" perfect swing, not "The" perfect swing.

- Give your students a suggestion list after every lesson; ask what they remembered from your time together.
- Remind students that over 60% of the shots in golf happen in the short game or from only 60 yards from the hole.
- The mental side of the game, along with the grip, posture, and stance, sometimes takes longer to learn than an understanding of the correct movements of the swing.
- Remember it's the eyes — both mental and physical — that control body movement. (You Must See First)
- Motion and feel are more important than position.
- We play golf with our nervous system. We must think before we move and move only after we think.
- Use lots of teaching aids; not only will students learn from them, but teaching aids make lessons more enjoyable.
- Teach students to play golf in a "state of grace."
- Do not over teach but encourage self-discovery. Use lots of pictures when coaching.
- Let students know that progress will come through practice. Be a cheerleader. Teach don't Preach!
- Let students know how often you would like to see them, and the things to do and practice between lessons.
- Let students know that being in good health and condition are important. When we are tired, we lose our ability to concentrate and pay attention.
- Self-image will sometimes slow progress down. Children are not afraid of making mistakes — adults are.
- Remind students that in a 4-hour round of golf there are only a few minutes of swing time.

RESEARCH

Dr. Ralph Mann and Jim Suttie, with computers have studied the golf swings of today's top professionals and after analyzing, their finding were:

BACKSWING:

The takeaway was a one-piece system, a "Body Shift." The trunk and the arms turn together with no wrist cock. The arms did not start first.

TOP OF BACK SWING:

The left arm bends more than 30 degrees at the top. The head is still, (it moves no more than 2 inches in any direction during the swing). At this point a lot of weight is on the right side.

STARTING FORWARD:

During the first move, the arms are not pulling, but are taken along by the body, and after that, it's all rotation unwinding the hips and upper body. By the time the hands have made any measurable movement, the hips and legs almost have returned to their address positions.

IMPACT:

The head stays behind the ball, nearly all of the body's movement is towards the target. All the golfer has to do is let the club come through. It is centrifugal force that works to square the clubface by impact. Research showed any attempt to control impact is futile, arms and wrists are not strong enough to control the speeding clubhead. Proper IMPACT is produced by a proper positioning of the club at the top of the swing and the proper early front swing move. At impact, the hands are slowing down, all the speed and power that the swing has produced is now in the clubhead.

FINISH:

The belly button should point left of the target, not directly at it as most people think. If the chest does face the target, it means that the hips have not cleared properly.

ONE SWING:

The research shows good players make the same swing with all clubs. A slight change in posture due to different length clubs and the length of the back swing are the only changes.

Tests and research conducted by *Centinela Medical Center at their Biomechanics Lab in Inglewood, California* were done in a scientific manner to analyze and identify which muscles were being used and when during a golf swing.

The findings were:

A. Both the left and right sides of the body play equal roles in providing power for the swing. The laboratory felt these findings may surprise some golf instructors who feel golf is a left-sided game. Tests do show there is equal emphasis from both sides of the body during the swing.

B. The hips initiate movement into the ball. The data shows the hip muscle activity is started before the upper body turns into the shot. The hips pull you through.

C. Less skilled players tend to get less than half the trunk rotation of a skilled player. The most noticeable difference seen on film when comparing amateurs to professionals is their lack of trunk rotation. Research showed without trunk rotation there is a loss of motion which enables the body segments to transmit maximum velocity to the clubhead at impact. Golfers give themselves a noticeable handicap by letting their available arc of motion diminish through lack of flexibility and by failing to realize the importance of Body Rotation. Power in golf can be achieved by rotating the body segments through space, and transferring energy from one segment to the next. When you diminish the space through which these segments move, then you *must use* more Muscle Power or effort to derive the same output.

D. Findings show that it's the large muscles in the body that supply most of the power in a golf swing. A muscle's power is in proportion to its cross-sectional area or size; meaning that the bigger it is, the more potential power it has.

    No matter how strong your wrists and forearms might be, they cannot substitute for the proper use of your hip muscles. (Research shows your hip muscles are the largest in the body and you must learn to use their potential power.)

E. Tests also show that less skilled golfers tend to swing the club primarily with the arms, while failing to use the power available to them in their truk, hips and legs. The golfer who is a "hands and arms" swinger loses a tremendous amount of potential power by failing to get a good body turn that makes use of the larger muscles.

    The research has given a keen appreciation for the contributions made by the trunk and the lower body, as it relates to what happens at impact. The lab results encourage all golfers to emphasize these parts of the body instead of only arms, hands and wrists.

F. When tests compared professionals with amateurs, the results showed skilled players use a much lower percentage of their muscular power at their swing. When the whole body is rotating, swinging the club takes less muscular effort. This is consistent with what the Biomechanics Lab has learned while investigating other sports such as tennis and basketball.

The National Golf Foundation's book *Exercise Fitness for Golf,* analyzes the golf swing and identifies the muscles which produce the swing.

For this book, the golf swing and muscle analysis was done by review of high speed film, by recording the electrical activity of muscles and by personal observation, by Bill Leary.

THEIR FINDINGS:

Backswing has three purposes:

1. To shift the weight of the body opposite the flight of the ball.
2. To put the muscles on stretch that will propel the club.
3. To move the clubhead as far away from the ball as possible; so the club can have the greatest distance over which to accelerate before impacting the ball.

In the backswing muscles of the trunk are rotating the upper body to the right, around the pelvis. Pectoralis major and deltoid muscles of the left side, the right trapezius and deltoid pull the arm into the back swing position.

When the backswing has been completed the muscles to be used to perform the swing are now on stretch and should be relaxed, not tight.

In the forward swing the muscles have three principle purposes:

1. Move the weight of the body laterally in the direction of flight.
2. Constantly accelerate the clubhead.

In order for the greatest amount of force to be transmitted to the clubhead, each muscle group must be contracted in an exacting sequence with the larger, slower muscles of the hips and truck acting first, followed by those of the shoulders and finally the wrist.

A good follow-through is essential to consistent golf and it has three objectives:

1. To reduce the force generated by the muscles.
2. To assure there is no additional muscular effort intended to end the swing that could interfere with momentum before the ball has left the clubface.
3. To assure that there is no additional muscular effort intended to end the swing that could change the desired arc of the down swing.

The following research and test were done by the Golf Society of Great Britain in the early 1960's. Their complete findings can be found in the book *The Search For The Perfect Swing*.

Power - A good golfer can generate up to "4 horse-power." This is surprisingly high power - and it leaves no doubt that the big muscles of the legs and trunk play a greater part in the top calss player's striking of the ball than those of his arms and hands.

Force - The force applied to the ball by the clubhead during impact in a full drive rises to a peak of about 2000 pounds - with an average of 1400.

Feel - When a golfer's brain can be said to have "felt" the impact of a shot the ball is already 15 yards away.

It takes 2/3 of a milisecond for the shock of impact to travel up the shaft from the clubface to the hands - and the ball is already in flight about 1/2 inch clear of the clubface. At least a further ten mili-seconds must elapse before the message gets to the golfer's brain. It would be at least another 1/5 of a second before orders from the golfer's brain could cause his hands to take any action to modify the stroke, and nothing can be done to affect the ball, which by this time would be 15 yards away.

Speed - The top class golfer may accelerate the clubhead about one hundred times as fast as the fastest sports car can accelerate: From the top of the backswing to 100 miles per hour at impact; all in as little as one-fifth of a second.

Traveling at 100 miles per hour, a driver head sends the ball away at about 135 miles per hour.

Off Line Shot - Pulls and pushes are straight shots in the wrong direction.

For every 1° the swing itself is off line - the Push or Pull will be 3½ yards from the intended line, on a 200 yard shot. A shot that is 20 yards off line, the direction of the swing must be 6° off line - quite a big error of swing.

Hooks and slices are caused by the clubface aiming, at impact, in a different direction from that in which it is being swung. These shots will go twice as far off line as pulls or pushes. The clubface that points only 1° off the direction in which it is swung, will send the ball 7 or 8 yards off line. The 20 yards off line shot needs less than a 3° mistake in face alignment.

What these Scientific facts mean in plain language is: What we all feel while making a stroke is not how we are hitting the ball, but *how we have already* hit it. This can only mean that in hitting a full drive, the player in effect puts his clubhead into orbit at 100 miles per hour around himself and "PERFORCE" because he can't do anything else - leaves the clubhead to hit the ball entirely on its own, in the path and at the speed he has already given it.

At the "moment of impact," the clubhead might just as well be connected to his hands by a number of strings holding it to the circle of its orbit, for all the effect he can have on it.

Any top-class player, in his swinging of a club, consistently manages to align his clubface at impact within 2° of the direction of his swing. That is pretty narrow bounds within which to confine natural human errors for a full length shot. To achieve this accuracy, system or swing just has to be as simple as possible.

The Fundamental theory of the swing: A good swing must have Speed, Accuracy, and the ability to repeat itself consistently. All possible sources of human error, liable to cause variations from swing to swing, must be reduced to a minimum. Any very complicated forms of movements are, therefore, to be avoided. To repeat itself consistently, the swing must be simple.

The fundamental approach offers this simple skeleton of a good swing: A circular movement of the hands around a fixed center, swinging in plane, with the club hinging in the same plane from the hands as it goes, and with the hands *not* necessarily applying any force themselves.

The golfer (Now Scientifically Proven) must find the most effective way of using the big muscles in the hip and legs to generate swinging momentum. To do so he must move his hips laterally. (Whatever else he also does with them.)

The Center Cannot Move, The Head Can

If the swing is to work in its simplest and most powerful form, the golfer must keep the center of his swing fixed. He must do so from at least the very beginning of the forward swing up to the moment of striking the ball.

A golf swing can work, after a fashion, even if the center is moved forward towards the hole during the downswing. But moving the center (which in effect means the whole body) during the forward swing reduces any player's abililty to generate the greatest possible clubhead speed into impact. It also makes the swings workings more complicated.

In the swings of top professionals any sudden shift forward in the position of the fixed center of the swinging action appears to take place only at the stage of the Reversal of swing direction at the top of the backswing. During the actual down, forward, and through swing, the center point stays still.

The center point of a swing is not the head; the center lies, for most players, somewhere in the middle of the chest just below the shoulders. In fact, as the hips are moving forward, with the hub or center held still, the good player's head may move slightly back and downward. In any normal shot the head will not move forward.

Research shows, if the center point is to remain fixed during the hip movement forward, the head must move back and down. Most good players do this, but not of course, by conscious effort.

Difficulties In Maintaining Plane

Research shows that there are only one or two specific points in the swing where things can very easily swing out of alignment or off plane; The takeway and the first movement of the downswing.

The clubhead's momentum on the backswing will have tended to take the clubhead back to whatever position the takeway started it towards.

One very important thing to realize about the forward swing, once the swing has gotten properly underway it will always tend to follow the plane it has set off in.

Scientists feel it can help a golfer to have in his mind, all the time, a clear uncomplicated picture of the basically simple movements he is using to govern all the complications of limbs, muscles and joints. This is where the idea of the whole swing working around a central hub may be very useful to him. The idea of a hub governing the swing from somewhere between the shoulders can make an excellent practical basis for trying to swing the club on plane.

Tests show that although the actual movements taking place at all the joints which the golfer uses are together quite complicated, the constant overall tendency will be for the swinging action itself to smooth out most of the complications of its own accord.

Any sort of swinging momentum of a golf club will try to move in the smoothest and simplest possible way. We do not, in any way, have to *force* the swing. On the contrary, the art of golf lies in *allowing* our swing to happen.

Backswing Findings

Scientists found the structural movements the golfer has to make during a sound swing will look quite complicated if taken bit by bit; and even more so if or when analyzed scientifically in terms of joints and muscle movements.

Research will show the exact opposite. The movements we need to make in order to reproduce a sound swing are really unexpectedly few and simple.

Scientists have broken the backswing down into five movements: (1) Turning of upper chest, (2) Raising of the arms, (3) Wrist cocking, (4) Hand and clubhead moving into plane, (5) The forearm and hand move together on the axis facing upwards.

Scientists found describing these movements *very much more* complicated than carrying them out. They will happen quite naturally if they are given the chance to. It seems certain that the correct top-of-backswing position is the successful coordination of the first foot or so of the swing. If this is achieved, the rest of the backswing will tend to follow naturally.

When this is not achieved, or if any other moves are deliberately or excessively used at this stage, the whole backswing is likely to be made *much more difficult* to complete correctly. This is why professionals often advise a "one piece-takeaway" or a "wide arc."

Forward Swing Findings

To investigate the workings of the swing scientifically, our team of research scientists fed information into a computer to carry out experiments in terms of mathematics alone. What the team found was the sequence of movements in the forward swing is really much simpler than in the backswing.

The basic timing of the sequence is: hub, unhinge, clubhead; or in human terms, body, hands, clubhead. The golf swing will actually generate power in the sequence of: legs, hips, trunk, upper chest and shoulders. There is *never* any unnecessary slack. From the toes to the clubhead everything happend or should happen in a *tight* sequence.

The general conclusion holds: That every part of the rotating and swinging system *must be pulled* around by the part nearer to the ground, until that part can no longer apply useful effort. In terms of a human golfer, the legs pull around the hips, the hips the trunk, the trunk the upper chest and shoulders, the shoulders the arms, the arms the hands, the hands the shaft, and the shaft the clubhead.

The primary power for the sound swing is going to come in sequence from the legs, hips, trunk and big muscles of the chest and back.

Through The Ball

Research findings show: In order to reproduce the actions through the ball that fit into the requirements of a sound swing, the golfer must do the following things: The main point the player will need to do is start the upper lever down and through the swing in plane.

It will be the hub action which will set the plane, pattern and timing of the swing at the ball. Thus, during the first stage, before the clubhead has been given enough momentum to follow the plane set for it in the downswing, the shoulder action must work in a way as to get the whole action moving in the plane required. Doing this may be difficult because of the tendency for the "right arm" and side, to take over control too soon.

Right Arm

Research shows the right arm should be reinforcing and supporting the swing. The right arm can most effectively contribute to the whole golf swing by (1) Reinforce and brace the swinging action of the upper lever, (2) To provide additional clubhead speed into impact, (3) To add both control and sensitivity to his clubhead, (4) To do what is required in #1, #2, #3, without upsetting the pattern or plane of the left arm swing.

To serve, reinforce, add extra power: control and sensitivity; but not to change or impose any right arm based pattern upon the swing.

Follow-Through

The follow-through is an inevitable continuation of the swinging action through the ball. It serves the purpose of absorbing the momentum of the body, arms and club left over after impact.

The primary power during the follow-through will be, of course, the momentum in the clubhead itself.

The aim of the swing is to transfer as much as possible, the momentum generated in the body and arms out into the clubhead at impact. So much momentum is absorbed by the clubhead, the clubhead now is pulling the swing into its follow-through against the resistance of the arms, body and legs.

How Muscles Work In Golf

The main power of the forward swing must come from positive muscle action. Muscles are not elastic, when stretched, they stay stretched, until they are told to contract. They are not themselves elastic. The back swing is not like winding up a big spring, it only puts the club on plane.

Another important property of muscles is that they can only pull, not push. In general, big muscles work at their greatest efficiency and give their greatest power when working comparatively slow; whereas small muscles give their peak performance when moving faster.

Scientists tell us, without even considering the detailed movements in a golf swing, they can make a fundamental and far-reaching statement about it. The muscles of the legs and hips constitute the main source of power in long driving.

Provided there is no slack higher up, an early thrust of the hips towards the hole will set the whole massive upper part of the system rotating as one unit about a horizontal axis through the pivot. This is the IDEAL movement with which to set the down swing going.

The hip movement is, therefore, neither a simple rotation nor a simple lateral movement, but a combination of both. It is a very powerful movement, and one that must be fully and correctly accomplished by anyone aspiring to hit the ball long distances.

If there is a secret of long driving, this is it. By doing things this way, we not only transfer energy efficiently, but actually ensure that the large muscles produce something near their maximum amount of power.

We can carry this argument ever further - and arrive at an important practical conclusion. The load can be effectively increased if we start the forward swing of the hips before the back swing of the club is complete.

All good golfers, in fact, do start their hips forward before the clubhead reaches the limit of its back swing, by over a tenth of a second. In fact, to allow this to happen is one of the two main purposes of having a backswing. The other is to put the club on the plane of the swing.

During the swing, power moves out into the clubhead and the hands and arms start to slow down in the impact area as the clubhead is speeding up.

Programming The Swing

Information is passed to the brain and used, together with memories stored from the results of previous experience, to come to a decision. This decision is coded in the form of nervous impulses and passed to the appropriate muscles which carry out the tasks required of them.

An Experiment in reaction time

A golfer is hitting drives into a net in a room, from which all daylight has been excluded, and which is lit by a single artificial light. It is rather a special one, because when it is switched off the light decays rapidly, indeed; for all practical purposes the room is instantly plunged into darkness. The golfer goes on hitting shot after shot, and, as a measure of how good each shot is, the speed of the ball and the point on the clubface, where contact is made, are recorded.

During some swings, however, the light is switched off. The golfer knows this is sometimes going to happen; but he doesn't know in which swing. When it does happen, he is to do whatever he can to stop his swing; or, if he can't do that, at least to change it by slowing down, by swinging over the top of the ball, or by mishitting it.

The object of the experiment is to find out by switching off the light at different points in the swing - at what stage is the golfer totally committed to his shot and quite unable to alter it in any way?

Well, where would you say was the point of no return? Clubhead a foot from the ball? Or two feet? Or halfway through the downswing? In fact, much earlier than any of these. Of all the many golfers tested, not one could in any way alter his stroke when the light went off after a point just barely into the downswing. Nearly all could actually stop the shot if the light went out during the backswing.

What this implies is that once any of us has fairly begun the forward swing, we can't correct or alter it in any way.

This may surprise golfers. It didn't surprise the scientists carrying out the test too much, because the time the down swing takes (0.2 to 0.25) is just about the minimum time required for the brain to perceive external signals, to give orders for the appropriate action, and for the muscles concerned to do something about it.

Correcting an error — only on the backswing

Should a golfer feel he has 'gone wrong' at any stage after his downswing has started, there is absolutely nothing he can do about it.

This is not to say that a shot which starts wrongly cannot be saved; but, to be saved, it must have gone wrong, and the news of this must have been passed to the brain earlier, sometime during the backswing.

He may not know this. He may well imagine that the whole process occurred in the downswing; but this is an illusion. The 'lights-out' experiment showed this up quite clearly. The golfers tested were asked to say when they thought the light had been switched off; and, without exception, they said it had gone out later than it actually did. For example, if the light went out at the beginning of the downswing, most thought it went out at about impact.

Clicking cameras and overhanging branches

Players often complain that a photographer, by taking a picture during their downswing, has distracted their concentration and spoiled their shot. Well, in those terms, it just couldn't happen. According to this experiment, any click during the downswing could not possibly affect the shot, and would probably not even register in the player's mind until the ball had gone. However, if the camera clicked during the backswing, then the player might be aware of it in time for it to upset his concentration; and he might imagine he heard it happen during the backswing.

Something readers may be familiar with - if you are playing from under a tree and you are aware of the possibility of hitting a branch near the top of your backswing, it is relatively easy, should you actually hit the branch, to stop your swing and try again. However, if you haven't noticed the branch, or if the possibility of hitting it has not occurred to you, you will find it difficult or impossible to stop.

The whole swing is programmed in advance

In the golf swing, the brain programs the whole series of events in advance. It sends pretty well all necessary instructions to the muscles before the movement actually starts. Once the operation is under way it is very difficult, and, after a certain stage, impossible to break into the system and alter it. And this, of course, is just what getting set up, concentrating, waiting for the right moment to swing is all about. The golfer must marshall all his thoughts before he swings; and to do this he will probably need to have one positive thought in his mind about what he is going to do during the swing.

A few checks before the swing; only one during it

It is not really possible to think of more than one or two things in any single swing -which is why beginners find it so difficult to learn, particularly if given too much instruction at once. It is also one reason why pros teach grip and stance first.

The first movement of the backswing, or the way you feel it, is also something that you can take time to prepare for; and this is important. So all good golfers, good or bad, should take advantage of the time available to get these things right. In competition some positive thought should be in his mind for every shot, if only to block out negative ones.

These positive thoughts can be almost anything. Interpreted literally, they may even be quite nonsensical. Yet, in so far as their object is to achieve some real practical effect by getting the player to aim at a 'feeling' of something imaginary or even impossible, they may make very good sense.

Always though, the player must have his key thought absolutely clear in his mind before he begins his swing.

Building up the beginner's program

In essence, we have been saying that before every shot the player has to make up his mind exactly what sort of stroke he needs to play, take up his position to hit the ball and then, by making a decision in his brain, switch on the programmed sequence of instructions to the muscles. The novice, of course, has no program to switch on, and his problem is to build one in his brain - to 'learn the golf swing.'

When the budding golfer starts to learn, he is aware of many separate feelings from various parts of his body. But gradually, after repeating the moves of the backswing a few thousand times, he becomes less aware of feelings from individual parts of the body and begins to gain a much more general impression of the whole movement. The size of this movement has probably then been increased to include the downswing; and again over a long period, and after many repitions, he 'feels' the swing as a unified movement.

Once a pupil has become reasonably competent, he must guard against giving too much consideration to movements of isolated parts of the body and too little to the continuity and rhythm of the whole movement. For this reason a visit to a professional tournament often helps golfers of all abilities. It isn't that you need look for particular technical points on the grip, the stance or anything else, but that a general sense of timing and flow rub off on to your own swing, at least for a time.

Seeing yourself on film has a similar effect, particularly if the film can be compared with one of an expert golfer.

Some of the following information comes from the research Marianne Torbert (a Ph.D. at Temple University) had in her book *Secrets To Success in Sports and Play*. Her information is invaluable and she should be thanked by all for her efforts to improve the way we play sports. I am sorry to report this wonderful book is out of print.

Frequently, participants as well as some coaches really have no idea about "why" things happen. There are countless "How to Books" that contain misconceptions based upon either folklore of sports or the unsubstained opinions of popular sports figures.

An understanding of the mechanics of skilled human movements requires a sound insight into the concepts of Newtonian Physics and some familiarity with anatomical structure of the body.

Trying to understand the partnership of the physical side and the mental aspects is a very real challenge. This understanding and application of mechanical principles can be transferred from one activity to another, whether it be little league, varsity athletics or weekend golf.

BALANCE

Balance is the foundation from which we initiate all movement. We cannot effectively develop force nor can we hope for accuracy, consistency or coordination without good balance.

Three Important Principles of Balance are:

1. Keep your weight centered over your base of support.

2. Increase the size of your foundation (base of support) - spread feet.

3. Lower your center of gravity or weight - bend knees.

A persons center of gravity is the point around which the body can be balanced. Center of gravity is found roughly behind the belly button in the lower back.

Instability occurs and a loss of balance starts when the center of gravity moves nearer or beyond the outer border of the base of support. When losing our balance, we will tend to start moving somewhat rapidly and without any conscious effort, since the pull of gravity will be adding to the *loss* of balance and our ability to create force (causing quick starts or change of direction).

To Improve Balance:

1. Bend knees. This will lower the center of gravity, allowing body weight to be adjusted over the base of support.
2. Increase the base of support - spread feet.
3. When moving - keep center of gravity over the base of support.
4. Build the abdominal muscles - they are extremely helpful in keeping the center of gravity over the base of support.

FORCE BUILD UP REQUIRES TIME AND DISTANCE

Some participants reduce the *time* and distance over which force is developed, believing that RUSHING will contribute to maximum force development. The confusion lies between getting the action done quickly or forcefully.

This misconception normally fades with experience. If the act is rushed it could substantially reduce force development.

The time and distance over which force develops can be increased by a weight transfer, opposition, lengthening the lever, and flattening the swing arc. The elimination of any of the above reduces force development.

Extraneous Movements may reduce or inhibit force production. Any movement that does not contribute directly to the movements objective is wasteful and may even require compensating efforts to counteract its effect. One of the goals of practice should be to reduce or eliminate any unnecessary movements.

Non Contributing Tension will retard the build up of force and is counterproductive. Reciprocal innervation is a process by which dual messages stimulate specific muscles to contract while the opposing muscle group receive a message to relax. This allows contraction to occur without resistance.

Often the beginner or one who has great desire to succeed develops a RESIDUAL NON PRODUCTIVE TENSION in the muscles that need to be relaxed. This excess tension inhibits the freedom and flow of movement.

Being aware of the effect of tension can help. You can learn to relax more. You can see even the highly skilled attempting to reduce their tension level. Practice swings, stretching, or a shake out of the body are all helpful.

A Good Follow Through insures maximum velocity and force at the point of impact. The complete and extended follow through assures that the slowing down process will not be initiated too early during the final part of the action phase. This means maximum velocity is still available at impact, release, or other time of need.

Opposition of the upper and lower body make it possible to have:

- Time and distance of motion
- Total muscle involvement
- Full stretch of the trunk
- Better Balance

An object will be accelerated in the direction of force of impact. If the direction of impact force is a "scoop" or "chop" the resulting path of the object will be different than if the direction of impact was to be level. In striking a ball, the force is applied directly through the center of gravity of the object.

The final weight transfer continues over a bent forward knee into the follow through. This allows for a gradual and smooth absorption of force. The bent knee also aids in keeping the center of gravity low and over the base of support thus avoiding a loss of balance that could negatively affect consistency and accuracy.

FORCE DEVELOPMENT

Normally originates from the body's center of gravity and it then flows outward toward the end of the involved extremity.

For force to develop, some portion of the body must be stabilized. This stabilized part acts as a brace against which the moving parts can push or pull - and also prevents the absorbtion of force that would occur if there were no stablization.

This role that stabilizers play in force production has been neglected or overlooked by many less experienced participants. For instance, many golfers are not aware of the role abdominal muscles play in the distance of their drive.

Good abdominal development is necessary for several important mechanical functions:

1. Balance can be controlled better if the area in which the center of gravity is found can be held firmly.

2. The rotation of the trunk is, in part, carried out by the abdominal muscles. These muscles help to hold the pelvis, allowing the trunk movements to occur.

3. *All* forceful moves of the legs are dependent upon a stable pelvic foundation against which to move.

4. Forceful movement of the upper limbs originate in the pelvic region of the trunk, requiring a stabilization of the pelvic area.

The abdominals stabilize the hips and create the anchor point around which the swing and weight transfer take place (anchor point or center of gravity). The abdominals play a similar role in other sports, such as soccer, to name one.

FLAT SPOT:

A proper weight transfer can contribute substantially to force build up. This shift of weight also assists in timing and accuracy since transferring the body weight from the back foot to the forward foot allows for a flattening of the swinging arc.

Without a proper weight transfer, the swings ARC tends to be too much of a circle.

A proper weight transfer allows for the swings ARC to have what is called a FLAT SPOT.

The flat spot occurs because your swing ARC will take your center of gravity as its center. As you shift weight, the center of gravity also shifts. So you make one ARC from your INITIAL CENTER of gravity and end up swinging around a second center of gravity position. These two ARC's OVERLAP, creating a single longer ARC with a flat spot caused by the shift of weight and changing CENTER OF GRAVITY.

(The center of gravity is moved slightly back and forth in a sound swing, *NEVER* up and down. This center of gravity also *NEVER* approaches the OUTER BORDER of the base of support.

This FLAT SPOT allows the highly skilled players to hit, release or expand *LATER* in the flattened arc pattern, increasing the time and distance over which force can be developed before contact. The flat spot can also help beginners whose timing may be less than perfect.

Some Closing Thoughts

We all can improve as instructors, but first it will be helpful to understand:
A. The golf swing is a "motor skill," and should be taught with the same approach as other motor skills. This means beginning with the simplest actions and then moving step by step to the more intricate motions.
B. A student should never go on to the next step until they have made progress with the initial fundamentals. Too often, students move along before they are really ready, never fully grasping the concept, and the learning experience is fragmented and impaired. They have not mentally graduated to the next step.
C. Our body will improve with work and properly supervised practice with a specific goal in mind.
D. The mind relates best to *images, movements, results,* and *feedback.* A mental image precedes every physical action that we perform.

The sequence for learning occurs in three stages:
1. Analytical or Intellectual
2. Conceptual
3. Creative

The game of golf can be easy to learn and easy to play when students progress through this sequence.

In all skill learning, there is a *short* period of *"intellectual or analytical"* learning. It is during this period that a student learns the fundamentals of grip, posture, alignment, ball position, and pre-shot routine. This is followed by the *"conceptual stage"* where the student learns the function of the body and the golf club. The intellectual and conceptual stages liberate the *"creative"* elements of a student, allowing them to play golf. To play good golf we need to use our imagination and creativity.

The sequence for student progess is:
1. Pre-Swing Mechanics
2. Golf Swing Concept
3. Creative Shot Making

- Your ability to make progress in golf will depend, for the most part, on the amount of time and effort you invest in the many challenges the game presents.

- You also must believe that it is how we mentally visualize the shot and swing beforehand, that can make a real difference in the quality of your game.

- Most, if not all, power in sports is a direct result of a transfer of weight, and golf is no exception. Keep in mind we cannot transfer weight with our hands and arms (*outside*) but the bigger muscles of the (*inside*) body can.

- We would like all of our swings to have Centrifugal Force, and when the *Inside is moving the Outside* Centrifugal Force will be present.

- Please start to remember the feel of your good swings, and try to repeat that feel the next time you swing. Do not think about the ball.

- Stay smooth when you play golf. Take your time, relax and play in the "*State of Grace.*" Your golf swing does not have to be fast or hard to have power.

- Have patience when your golf is not what you would like it to be. Your game will come and go, it is the nature of golf. Have patience when your progress seems slow.

- Find yourself a good golf instructor that you can trust and work with him/her on a regular basis.

- Last, I hope you find our ideas and point of view helpful, and that they lead to more enjoyment when playing this game we all love.

Michael Hebron

SUGGESTED READINGS

Drawing on The Right Side of The Brain
by Betty Edwards

Exercise Fitness For Golf
National Golf Foundation

Inner Game of Golf
By Tim Gallow

One Move to Better Golf
by Carl Lohren

Bobby Jones on Golf
by Bobby Jones

The Full Swing
by Jack Nicklaus

Golf is My Game
by Bobby Jones

The Modern Fundamentals of Golf
by Ben Hogan

On Learning Golf
by Percy Boomer

Power Golf
by Ben Hogan

Better Golf Without Practice
by Alex Morrison

5 Days to Golfing Excellence
by Chuck Hogan

A New Way to Better Golf
by Alex Morrison

The Search for the Perfect Swing
by A. Cochran & John Stobbs

The Four Magic Moves to Winning Golf
by Joe Dante

30 Exercises for Better Golf
by Frank W. Jobe, M.D.

The Venturi Analysis
by K. Venturi

Golf in The Kingdom
by Michael Murphy

The Golf Secret
by H.A. Murray

Maximum Golf
by John Schlee

For information concerning

Mike Hebron's

WORKSHOPS / SEMINARS

CLINICS or PRIVATE LESSONS

write:

SMITHTOWN LANDING COUNTRY CLUB
495 Landing Avenue
Smithtown, New York 11787

or call:

516 - 360-7618